GW00787958

Instant Pot Cookbook

A Comprehensive Instant Pot Pressure Cooker Cookbook with 110 Amazing Recipes for Healthy, Fast, and Delicious Meals

Vanessa Olsen

Copyright 2016 by Vanessa Olsen - All rights reserved.

This document is geared towards providing exact and reliable information in regards to the topic and issue covered. The publication is sold with the idea that the publisher is not required to render accounting, officially permitted, or otherwise, qualified services. If advice is necessary, legal or professional, a practiced individual in the profession should be ordered.

- From a Declaration of Principles which was accepted and approved equally by a Committee of the American Bar Association and a Committee of Publishers and Associations.

In no way is it legal to reproduce, duplicate, or transmit any part of this document in either electronic means or in printed format. Recording of this publication is strictly prohibited and any storage of this document is not allowed unless with written permission from the publisher. All rights reserved.

The information provided herein is stated to be truthful and consistent, in that any liability, in terms of inattention or otherwise, by any usage or abuse of any policies, processes, or directions contained within is the solitary and utter responsibility of the recipient reader. Under no circumstances will any legal responsibility or blame be held against the publisher for any reparation, damages, or monetary loss due to the information herein, either directly or indirectly.

Respective authors own all copyrights not held by the publisher.

The information herein is offered for informational purposes solely, and is universal as so. The presentation of the information is without contract or any type of guarantee assurance.

The trademarks that are used are without any consent, and the publication of the trademark is without permission or backing by the trademark owner. All trademarks and brands within this book are for clarifying purposes only and are the owned by the owners themselves, not affiliated with this document.

ISBN: 1537388088
ISBN-13: 978-1537388083

Table of Contents

Introduction

Pressure cooking is the best way to prepare every meal - breakfast, lunch, and dinner. Food retains 80-90% of its nutritional value, and meals that ordinarily take hours are done in half the time. If you're a busy person who wants to eat healthier, you need a pressure cooker.

But, which pressure cooker should you get? While stovetop cookers have been around forever, electric ones are more convenient and safer. The Instant Pot specifically offers automatic cooking programs for meals like Soup, Poultry, and Yogurt, and is the safest pressure cooker out there. There are a lot of buttons, but we break it all down for you right away, and explain how to clean the Instant Pot.

The bulk of this book is made up of recipes. They are especially designed for the Instant Pot and are easy to follow, so even if you've only ever used a microwave, you'll be able to use the Instant Pot in no time. Starting with breakfast, you'll learn how to make chicken, beef, seafood, side dishes, ethnic food, vegan dishes, and desserts. Let's get started!

Chapter 1

What Is Pressure Cooking?

Pressure cooking has a long history, with the first pressure cooker dating back to 1679. The inventor believed that by raising the pressure in a cooking vessel, he could turn meat bones into jelly. He was right, but the cooker had a habit of exploding, and it was too expensive for most people to buy. By the time of Napoleon, another gentleman responded to the French army's request for a way to carry fresh food over a long time and long distances, and adapted the pressure cooker into the pressure canner.

For years, pressure canners were used by large companies, and not by regular Joe's. That changed in 1938 when the first small pressure cooker - about the size of a saucepan - entered circulation. People discovered they could cook just about anything in their pressure cooker, even cheap, tough cuts of meat, and get fall-off-the-bone tender dishes. From that time to today, pressure cookers have grown in popularity and been adapted from cookers used on the stove to electric cookers with automatic programs.

What makes pressure cooking so great? Here are just a few reasons:

- It's the healthiest way to prepare food - pressure cooking retains the most nutritional value of any food you cook.
- It makes certain foods easier to digest - think grains and beans, which can cause problems for many people.
- It's super fast - you can cook rice in just a few minutes and food that usually needs hours and hours of cooking can get done in less than ½ the time.

There are some terms you should know that apply to every pressure cooker. It will make choosing and using your cooker much easier.

- <u>PSI</u> - this measures the pressure in the cooker. Low PSI is anywhere from 6-8, while high PSI goes from 13-15. Certain foods should only be cooked at low pressure, and a recipe should specify.

- <u>Release</u> - when a pressure cooker has finished cooking something, all that pressure has to go somewhere. There are several ways to release pressure. Naturally release is when you turn off the cooker (either by removing it from the stove, unplugging it, or hitting "Cancel") and wait for the pressure to come down by itself. Quick-release is when you use the steam release handle and vent the pressure yourself, being careful to not get a faceful of scalding steam. For stovetop cookers, some people refer to a cold-water method, which is when you run the cooker under cold water to bring down the pressure extremely quickly, but that can be dangerous, and it isn't something you should concern yourself with for this book.

- <u>Minimum liquid</u> - there are some exceptions, but in order to work, a pressure cooker needs a minimum amount of liquid. It varies depending on the cooker size, but generally, ½ cup to 1 cup of water is necessary.

- <u>Secure/lock the lid</u> - before you start a pressure cooker, you always need to make sure the steam valve is in the locked position. Most electric cookers won't even start building pressure unless it's locked, but for stovetop ones, you will hear a hissing that lets you know the lid is not secure.

Chapter 2

Choosing a Pressure Cooker

When you're choosing a pressure cooker, think about how you cook now and what you would like to do differently. Do you want to cook healthier food, but without having to always buy the best - and most expensive - ingredients at the store? Do you want to speed up the cooking process? Luckily, no matter what pressure cooker you get, it will result in healthy, quick-cooking food. However, not all pressure cookers are equal.

The fastest pressure cookers are still stovetop cookers. Electric ones just aren't able to get up to the same PSI as stovetop. However, there's a lot more hands-on work with stovetop cookers, and only about a 10-minute difference in terms of speed. Electric cookers are also more convenient and safer, with the Instant Pot in particular hitting all the marks. Here are just a few reasons why you should choose an Instant Pot cooker over other electric brands:

- Built-in programs for Soup, Meat/Stew, Rice, and so on
- Easily-adjustable time settings
- Safety features that prevent too much steam build-up, protect against leaks, or accidentally starting the cooker without the lid
- Exceptional stainless-steel pots built for durability
- Dishwasher-safe parts ensure easy clean-up

The Instant Pot

There are currently three types of Instant Pots available in sizes from 5-8 quarts. The first is the 6-in-1, which has functions for sauté, warming, steaming, cooking rice, slow cooking, and pressure cooking. The 7-in-1 includes all the former, but has a new program for making yogurt. The latest Instant Pot - called the Instant Pot Smart - allows you to monitor cooking using a smart-device app. It also offers additional cooking programs and more safety features. Of the three, it is the most expensive. In terms of size, most families of four would do well with a 6-quart, which can fit a whole chicken.

Chapter 3

How Does The Instant Pot Work?

The Instant Pot has a relatively simple construction. The only parts you need to concern yourself with are the inner pot, which is where the food goes, the parts of the lid, and the control panel. The lid is sealed with a gasket, also called the sealing ring. It is removable and needs to be cleaned and eventually be replaced. The steam release handle needs to cover the steam release in order to lock the lid, while the float valve and exhaust valve are there to prevent too much pressure build-up. The last part, the control panel, has all the buttons you need to operate the Instant Pot.

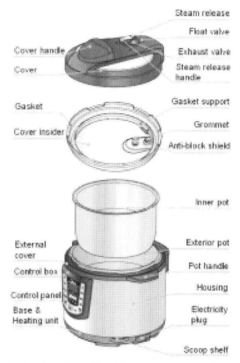

Instant Pot – Electric Pressure Cooker

Sauté: You use this function with the lid off and do anything you would with a skillet, like browning meat and cooking garlic, onion, and other aromatics.

Adjust: Hit adjust once for browning on the "sauté" function, and twice for simmering.

Slow Cook: This turns the Instant Pot into a slow cooker.

Pressure: Choose low or high pressure.

Yogurt: Choose this for making yogurt.

The "-" and "+" buttons: This adjusts the time, which you can adjust after hitting "Yogurt" or one of the other 8 cooking programs.

Keep Warm/Cancel: This turns off your pressure cooker or cancels a function if you hit the wrong one. When a cooking program ends, it automatically goes to Keep Warm. You can adjust the Keep Warm temperature using the Adjust button to normal/145-degrees, less/133-degrees, or more/167-degrees.

Manual: You'll be using this button a lot. Hit this button when you want to select a pressure and choose your own cooking time.

Soup: This automatic program is for high pressure, 30 minutes. Adjust time using the Adjust button.

Meat/Stew: Automatic program for high pressure, 35 minutes.

Beans/Chili: Automatic program for high pressure, 30 minutes.

Poultry: Automatic program for high pressure, 15 minutes.

Rice: White rice program for low pressure. It adjusts its own cooking time depending on the amount of rice and water.

Multi-grain: Automatic program for high pressure, 40 minutes.

Porridge: Automatic program for high pressure, 20 minutes.

Steam: Automatic program for high pressure, 10 minutes.

Timer: For the Instant Pot with this button, you can delay cooking. First hit the cooking function you want, hit timer, and then adjust time with the "-" or "+."

Using the Pot

When you're ready to make food, you should know there are a few ways to use it. You can put food right in the pot or use a steamer basket, which keeps food from touching the bottom of the pressure cooker. You can also use oven-safe baking dishes that fit in the cooker to make cakes and casseroles. For certain dishes, you have to wrap them in foil first. The recipe will let you know how best to prepare the food and if you need to wrap anything.

Remember, if you're filling the pot directly, only fill ⅔ of the way full. Filling it too full, especially if you're cooking a frothy food like pasta, oatmeal, or beans, the steam valve will get blocked. Another thing to keep in mind is you can't use the Instant Pot as a pressure canner, except for jams, pickles, and yogurt in jars.

With an Instant Pot, you can either quick-release by opening the steam valve or letting the pressure decrease naturally. Whichever you do, hit "Cancel" first or unplug the cooker.

.

Chapter 4

Cleaning the Instant Pot

To keep your Instant Pot in good shape, you need to clean it after each use. The inner pot at least should be cleaned. It's dishwasher safe, but it's easy to wipe it clean by hand, too, because it's stainless steel. Make sure to use a soft sponge, nothing abrasive. It's also a good idea to wash the gasket and lid every time. To wash the gasket, remove it from the lid, and wash with soap and warm water. It should not go in the dishwasher. If the gasket starts to smell or stain, you should soak it in hot water and soap for 15 minutes. Eventually, you'll need to buy a replacement gasket.

When you make rice, pasta, oatmeal, or other foods that get frothy, you should clean the exhaust valve. Take off the cover and clean using something thin that won't break, so do *not* use a toothpick.

The last thing to remember is to store the pressure cooker without the lid. Keeping the lid on traps odors, which is gross. Let the cooker air out.

Chapter 5

Breakfast

Homemade Vanilla Yogurt

Makes: 2-3 quarts
Time: About 12 hours

Making homemade yogurt has never been easier when you use the Instant Pot. The yogurt has a delicate vanilla flavor that's not too sweet, and easily customizable with fruit, nuts, and anything else you would like. You'll notice the recipe calls for you to strain the yogurt for ½-1 hour using nut milk bags. This is to help form a creamier, less runny yogurt.

Ingredients:

1 gallon 2% milk
½ cup yogurt starter (plain yogurt) with active cultures
3 tablespoons powdered milk
2 tablespoons pure vanilla extract
1 vanilla bean

Directions:

1. Pour all the milk into your Instant Pot.
2. Add the powdered milk and stir well.
3. Secure the lid on the Instant Pot and plug it in.
4. Select the "yogurt" setting.
5. Keep pressing "adjust" until you reach "boil."
6. The boil takes about an hour, after which you unplug the cooker and carefully remove the lid to let the milk cool to 115-degrees F.
7. When that temperature is reached, add the yogurt starter and vanilla extract.

8. Lock the lid and select "yogurt."
9. After 8 hours, pour the yogurt into nut milk bags (which you can find on Amazon) and strain for ½-1 hour.
10. When time is up, put the yogurt back into the Instant Pot and add the seeds from the vanilla bean. Mix thoroughly.
11. Put the yogurt into mason jars and refrigerate overnight.
12. When you're ready to enjoy, add any sweeteners, fruit, granola, or whatever else you like with your yogurt!

Nutritional Info (1/10 of recipe):

Total calories - 218
Protein - 14
Carbs - 20
Fiber - 0
Fat - 8

Steel-Cut Oats

Serves: 3-4
Time: 6-7 minutes

Oats are one of the best breakfasts you could have. They're full of fiber, so a bowl keeps you full till lunchtime, so you aren't snacking your way through the morning. If you've been making oats in the microwave or waiting by the stovetop, you'll be overjoyed at the speed and quality of the Instant Pot's steel-cut oatmeal.

Ingredients:
2 cups of water
1 cup steel-cut oats
Pinch of salt
Milk
Sugar

Directions:

1. Pour 1 cup of water into the Instant Pot and lower in the trivet.
2. In a heatproof bowl, mix 2 cups of water, oats, and salt.
3. Set on top of the trivet and lock the pressure cooker lid.
4. Select the "Manual" setting and cook for at least 6 minutes, but no more than 7.
5. Heat a cup or so of milk (depending on how much you want) in the microwave.
6. When the oats are done, scoop into individual serving bowls.
7. Pour milk on top and add sugar before serving.

Nutritional Info (¼ recipe):

Total calories - 155
Protein - 4
Carbs - 28

Fiber - 2
Fat - 3

Easy Soft-Boiled Egg Breakfast

Serves: 4
Time: 4 minutes

Soft-boiled eggs are a delicious way to get a jolt of protein in the morning, especially when served on a perfectly-toasted English muffin. For this Instant Pot recipe, all you need are eggs, a steamer basket, and canning lids.

Ingredients:

4 eggs
Two toasted English muffins
Salt and pepper to taste

Directions:

1. Pour 1 cup of water into the Instant Pot and insert the steamer basket.
2. Put four canning lids into the basket before placing the eggs on top of them, so they stay separated.
3. Secure the lid.
4. Press the "steam" setting and choose 4 minutes.
5. When ready, quick-release the steam valve.
6. Take out the eggs using tongs and dunk them into a bowl of cold water.
7. Wait 1-2 minutes.
8. Peel and serve with one egg per half of a toasted English muffin. Season with salt and pepper.

Nutritional Info (1 egg + ½ English muffin):

Total calories - 139   Fiber - 2
Protein - 9   Fat - 6
Carbs - 14

Maple-Syrup Quinoa

Serves: 4-5
Time: 11 minutes

Quinoa is one of the few complete proteins, making it a great superfood, and it doesn't have to be only savory. This breakfast quinoa is sweetened with maple syrup and vanilla, and can be served with add-ins like fresh fruit and nuts.

Ingredients:

2 ¼ cups water
1 ½ cups uncooked, rinsed quinoa
2 tablespoons maple syrup
½ teaspoon vanilla
¼ teaspoon cinnamon
Pinch of salt

Directions:

1. Add the water, quinoa, maple syrup, vanilla, cinnamon, and salt to the Instant Pot.
2. Select "Manual" and then "high pressure."
3. Choose the 1 minute cook-time.
4. When ready, turn off the pressure cooker and wait 10 minutes.
5. Quick-release the rest of the pressure.
6. Using a fork, fluff the quinoa.
7. Serve with milk, fruit, nuts, and/or more maple syrup if necessary.

Nutritional Info (⅕ of recipe):

Total calories - 213   Fiber - 2
Protein - 7   Fat - 3
Carbs - 41

French Toast Bake

Serves: 4
Time: 35 minutes

You don't have to go out for breakfast to get really good French toast. A dish that's notorious to get just right is made easy in the Instant Pot, and you'll want to make it again and again. Buy some cinnamon-raisin bread, let it go stale, and you'll be ready to make a delicious French-toast bake the whole family will love.

Ingredients:

3 big, beaten eggs
3 cups stale cinnamon-raisin bread, cut into cubes
1 ½ cups water
1 cup whole milk
2 tablespoons maple syrup
1 teaspoon butter
1 teaspoon sugar
1 teaspoon pure vanilla extract

Directions:

1. Pour the water into your Instant Pot and lower in the steam rack.
2. Grease a 6-7 inch soufflé pan.
3. In a bowl, mix milk, vanilla, maple syrup, and eggs.
4. Add the bread cubes and let them soak for 5 minutes.
5. Pour into the pan, making sure the bread is totally submerged.
6. Set in the pressure cooker.
7. Hit "Manual" and adjust the time to 15 minutes on "high pressure."
8. Quick-release the pressure when time is up.
9. Sprinkle the top with sugar and broil in the oven for 3 minutes.

Nutritional Info (¼ of recipe):

Total calories -183   Fiber - 0
Protein - 8   Fat - 3
Carbs - 21

Cheesy Sausage Frittata

Serves: 2-4
Time: 40 minutes

Cooked on low pressure, eggs and sausage blend with cheese for a hearty, hot breakfast that will leave you ready to take on whatever kind of day you have ahead of you. Frittatas are flexible, so you can add bacon and onion if you'd like.

Ingredients:

1 ½ cups water
4 beaten eggs
½ cup cooked ground sausage
¼ cup grated sharp cheddar
2 tablespoons sour cream
1 tablespoon butter
Salt to taste
Black pepper to taste

Directions:

1. Pour water into the Instant Pot and lower in the steamer rack.
2. Grease a 6-7 inch soufflé dish.
3. In a bowl, whisk the eggs and sour cream together.
4. Add cheese, sausage, salt, and pepper. Stir.
5. Pour into the dish and wrap tightly with foil all over.
6. Lower into the steam rack and close the pot lid.
7. Hit "Manual," and then 17 minutes on "low pressure."
8. Quick-release the pressure.
9. Serve hot!

Nutritional Info:

Total calories - 282
Protein - 16
Carbs - 1

Fiber - 0
Fat - 12

Creamy Strawberry Oatmeal

Serves: 1
Time: 20 minutes

This simple oatmeal for one only has five ingredients, but packs in almost 9 grams of protein. You can easily double the recipe to serve more people, and add toppings like nuts, seeds, dried coconut, and so on. You can also use fresh, frozen, or dried strawberries.

Ingredients:

⅔ cup whole milk
⅓ cup rolled oats
2 tablespoons strawberries
½ teaspoon sugar
1 pinch of salt

Directions:

1. Pour 2 cups of water into the Instant Pot and lower in the steamer basket.
2. Mix the milk, strawberries, oats, and salt in a small bowl.
3. Put the bowl into the pressure cooker and lock the lid.
4. Hit "Manual" and then 10 minutes on "high pressure."
5. When the timer goes off, hit "Cancel" and wait for the pressure to go down.
6. When the pressure is gone, open the lid and stir.
7. Serve with sugar and a sprinkle of cinnamon, if desired.

Nutritional Info:

Total calories - 207
Protein - 8.6
Carbs - 28.3

Fiber - 2.8
Fat - 7.3

Creamy Banana Oatmeal

Serves: 4
Time: 18 minutes

Got very ripe bananas? Make this awesome oatmeal with steel-cut oats. It's a very rich-tasting oatmeal thanks to the half-and-half, so feel free to eat this cold for a quick dessert later if you have any leftovers.

Ingredients:

2 ¼ cups water
½ cup steel-cut oats
2 very ripe, chopped bananas
½ cup packed light brown sugar
¼ cup half-and-half
2 teaspoons vanilla extract
½ teaspoon ground cinnamon
¼ teaspoon salt

Directions:

1. Mix oats, bananas, brown sugar, vanilla, salt, and cinnamon with 2 ¼ cups and pour into the Instant Pot.
2. When the brown sugar dissolves, close the lid.
3. Select "Manual" and then 18 minutes at "high pressure."
4. When time is up, hit "Cancel" and wait for the pressure to come down on its own.
5. When time is up, carefully open the cooker.
6. Stir in the half-and half, and enjoy!

Nutritional Info (¼ recipe):

Total calories - 130
Protein - 3
Carbs - 26

Fiber - 2
Fat - 3

Ham, Apple, and Grits Casserole

Serves: 4-6
Time: 22 minutes

If you're having people over for brunch, this is a great recipe to use. It's unusual enough to impress everyone, but has familiar ingredients that won't be a problem for pickier eaters.

Ingredients:

8 ounces of chopped Canadian bacon
4 sliced scallions
2 big, beaten eggs
¾ cups instant grits
½ cup shredded cheddar cheese
1 peeled and chopped green apple
2 tablespoons butter
1 teaspoon dried thyme

Directions:

1. Turn your Instant Pot to "Sauté" to melt the butter.
2. Add the ham, stirring, and cook for 1 minute.
3. Toss in the scallions, thyme, and apples.
4. Stir and cook for another minute.
5. Move everything to a bowl and set aside.
6. Hit "Cancel" on the Instant Pot.
7. Wipe down the inside of the pot with a paper towel.
8. Turn "Sauté" back on and pour in 3 cups of water.
9. When boiling, add the grits.
10. Whisk constantly until the grits are thick.
11. Hit "Cancel" again.
12. Move the grits to the bowl with the other cooked ingredients.
13. Let the grits cool for 10 minutes while you clean out the cooker.
14. Pour in another 2 cups of water.
15. Put in the trivet.
16. Stir the cheese and eggs into the grits' bowl.
17. Pour into a greased 2-quart, round baking dish and cover with foil.
18. Lower into the Instant Pot.

19. Secure the lid and hit "Manual," and then 22 minutes on "high pressure."
20. Quick-release the pressure when time is up.
21. Cool before serving.

Nutritional Info (⅙ recipe):

Total calories - 157
Protein - 12.3
Carbs - 8.9
Fiber - .5
Fat - 7.7

Savory Breakfast Porridge

Serves: 4
Time: 1 hour

A lot of breakfast foods, especially porridge, are sweet. If you're a person who frequently eats leftovers for breakfast, this rice porridge with scallions, soy sauce, and egg will satisfy that savory tooth.

2 cups chicken broth
2 cups water
4 eggs
4 chopped scallions
½ cup rinsed and drained white rice

1 tablespoon sugar
1 tablespoon olive oil
2 teaspoons soy sauce
½ teaspoon salt
Black pepper

Directions:

1. Pour water, broth, sugar, salt, and rice into the Instant Pot.
2. Close the lid.
3. Hit "Porridge" and 30 minutes on "high pressure."
4. While that cooks, heat oil in a saucepan.
5. Crack in the eggs one at a time, so they aren't touching each other.
6. Cook until the whites become crispy on the edges, but the yolks are still runny.
7. Sprinkle on salt and pepper.
8. When the Instant Pot timer goes off, hit "Cancel" and wait for the pressure to go down on its own.
9. If the porridge isn't thick enough, hit "Sauté" and cook uncovered for 5-10 minutes.
10. Serve with scallions, soy sauce, and an egg per bowl.

Nutritional Info (¼ recipe):

Total calories - 214
Protein - 10
Carbs - 24

Fiber - 1
Fat - 2

Blueberry Croissant Pudding

Serves: 7
Time: 40 minutes

Bread puddings for breakfast are awesome. This one is designed for breakfast, since it uses croissants for the bread and blueberries as a topping.

Ingredients:

3 big, cut-up croissants
One 8-ounce package softened cream cheese
2 eggs
1 cup blueberries
1 cup milk
⅔ cup sugar
1 teaspoon vanilla

Directions:

1. Put the croissants and blueberries in a heat-safe bowl you know fits in the Instant Pot.
2. In a separate bowl, mix cream cheese, eggs, sugar, and vanilla.
3. Add milk and mix again.
4. Pour over the croissants and rest for 20 minutes.
5. When ready, put the bowl in the Instant Pot and lock the lid.
6. Press "Manual," and then "high pressure" for 20 minutes.
7. When time is up, hit "Cancel" and then quick-release.
8. Serve!

Nutritional Info (1 / 7 recipe):

Total calories - 263
Protein - 8
Carbs - 40

Fiber - 2
Fat - 18

Chapter 6

Chicken

<u>Sticky Sesame Chicken</u>

Serves: 4
Time: About 30 minutes

You'll have to resist licking your fingers after enjoying this chicken dish. The chicken of choice is chicken thigh fillets, which stay more moist than chicken breasts, while the sauce is a mix of hoisin, sweet chili sauce, garlic, ginger, rice vinegar, and sesame seeds. Serve with rice, noodles, or veggies for a complete meal.

<u>Ingredients:</u>

6 boneless chicken thigh fillets
4 peeled and crushed garlic cloves
5 tablespoons hoisin sauce
5 tablespoons sweet chili sauce
½ cup chicken stock
1 chunk of peeled, grated fresh ginger
1 ½ tablespoons sesame seeds
1 tablespoon rice vinegar
1 tablespoon soy sauce

<u>Directions:</u>

1. Spread chicken thighs flat and place them into the Instant Pot.
2. Whisk garlic, ginger, chili sauce, hoisin, vinegar, sesame seeds, broth, and soy sauce into a sauce.
3. Pour over chicken and stir.

4. Select "Manual," and then 15 minutes on "high pressure."
5. When time is up, hit "Cancel" and wait for a natural pressure release.
6. When all the pressure is gone, open up the cooker and serve the chicken with rice.

Nutritional Info (¼ serving):

Total calories - 428
Protein - 30
Carbs - 52.9
Fiber - 1
Fat - 9

Chicken & Dumplings

Serve: 8
Time: 55 minutes

When it's cold and unpleasant outside, I crave something hot and comforting. This chicken & dumplings recipe hits the spot. The chicken and broth are cooked first, and then the homemade dumplings are added later. Use chicken thighs for the most tender meat.

3 ½ cups chicken broth
8 chicken thighs
4 chopped celery stalks
4 tablespoons butter
3 peeled and chopped carrots
2 chopped onions
2 tablespoons cornstarch
½ cup flour
½ cup whole milk
Salt + pepper

1 ¾ cups flour
1 cup whole milk
¼ cup cornmeal
3 tablespoons melted butter
1 tablespoon baking powder
½ teaspoon salt
¼ teaspoon pepper

Directions:

1. Turn the Instant Pot to "Sauté" and add the butter from the first ingredient list.
2. Season chicken with salt, pepper, and coat in flour.
3. When the butter is hot, brown the chicken in batches on both sides.
4. Set chicken aside.
5. Add onions, celery, and carrots, and cook for 3 minutes.
6. Pour in chicken broth and add the browned chicken back to the pot.
7. Sprinkle with salt and pepper.

8. Lock the pot lid.
9. Hit "Manual" and cook for 11 minutes at "high pressure."
10. Look to the second ingredient list to make the dumplings.
11. Mix cornmeal, baking powder, flour, salt, and pepper.
12. Pour in the milk and melted butter and mix until just moistened.
13. When the Instant Pot timer goes off, hit "Cancel" and quick-release.
14. Pour in milk (from the first ingredient list) and mix.
15. In a separate bowl, mix ½ cup of the hot broth with cornstarch.
16. Pour back into the Instant Pot and stir to thicken.
17. Turn the pot back to "Sauté."
18. In tablespoons, put dumplings into the pot. They should be separated from each other and submerged in the liquid.
19. Cook for 12-15 minutes with the lid on, but not locked. Leave it on a little lopsided, so hot air can escape.
20. When the dumplings have grown twice their original size, they're done.
21. Take the meat off the chicken bones and add back to the pot.
22. Serve!

Nutritional Info (⅛ serving):

Total calories - 543
Protein - 25
Carbs - 40
Fiber - 2
Fat - 14

Spicy-Honey BBQ Chicken Wings

Serves: 4 (for dinner)
Time: About 25-30 minutes

You'll want to lick your fingers after devouring these spicy-sweet chicken wings that have both a cooking sauce *and* basting sauce. The first sauce and frozen chicken wings cook quickly in the pressure cooker before you finish them off in a broiler, just to give them that crispy exterior.

Ingredients:

2 pounds frozen chicken wings
¾ cup honey BBQ sauce
½ cup apple juice
½ cup water
½ cup brown sugar
2 teaspoons paprika
1 teaspoon black pepper
1 teaspoon crushed red pepper
½ teaspoon basil
½ teaspoon cayenne

¾ cup honey BBQ sauce
½ cup apple juice
½ cup brown sugar
2 teaspoons paprika
1 teaspoon black pepper
1 teaspoon crushed red pepper
½ teaspoon cayenne
½ teaspoon basil
½ teaspoon liquid smoke

Directions:

1. Mix all the ingredients in the first list in the Instant Pot.
2. Select "Manual," and then choose "high pressure" for 10 minutes.
3. When the timer beeps, quick-release the pressure.
4. Arrange the wings on a baking sheet.
5. The basting sauce is the same as the pressure-cooker sauce, just with

liquid smoke added.
6. Baste and broil for 7 minutes.
7. Turn the wings over, baste again, and broil for another 7 minutes.
8. Broil for another 4 minutes or so, basting halfway through.
9. Serve with a side dish like potatoes, corn, or coleslaw.

Nutritional Info (½ pound wings):

Total calories - 360
Protein - 34
Carbs - 16
Fiber - 0
Fat - 8

Balsamic Chicken Thighs

Serves: 2
Time: About 20 minutes

Balsamic vinegar is one of the best marinades for just about anything, including chicken thighs. There are so many kinds, and you can use whatever you want, just make sure it's a good quality. These balsamic-thighs are so easy, you just mix everything in a bag, cook some aromatics, and throw everything into the Instant Pot for just 15 minutes. It's a perfect weekday meal.

Ingredients:

1 pound boneless, skinless chicken thighs
½ cup balsamic vinegar
⅓ cup cream sherry wine
2 tablespoons chopped cilantro
2 tablespoons olive oil
2 tablespoons minced green onion
1 ½ teaspoons minced garlic
1 teaspoon dried basil
1 teaspoon garlic powder
1 teaspoon Worcestershire sauce
½ teaspoon black pepper

Directions:

1. Mix basil, salt, garlic, pepper, sherry, Worcestershire, onion, and vinegar in a plastic bag.
2. Add chicken and squish around, so the chicken becomes completely coated.
3. Turn your Instant Pot on and select "sauté."
4. Pour in the olive oil and cook the minced garlic, stirring, until fragrant.
5. Turn the pot to "Poultry" and pour in the chicken and sauce.
6. Secure the lid.
7. The "Poultry" setting defaults to 15 minutes, which is the correct length of time for this recipe.
8. When it beeps, quick-release the pressure.

9. Serve with chopped cilantro and a side dish like rice or veggies.

Nutritional Info (½ pound thighs):

Total calories - 210
Protein - 14
Carbs - 10
Fiber - 0
Fat - 12

Half-Hour Chicken Cacciatore

Serves: 4-6
Time: 30 minutes

This classic chicken dish is rich, but healthy. There's no cream or other unnecessary fats - it's just chicken, tomatoes, olives, and spices. Eat like an Italian, but without the long cooking times that tend to accompany that style of cuisine.

Ingredients:

6-8 bone-in chicken drumsticks
1 cup chicken stock
1 chopped yellow onion
1 can whole stewed tomatoes in a puree

1 bay leaf
½ cup pitted black olives
1 teaspoon dried oregano
1 teaspoon garlic powder

Directions:

1. Turn on your Instant Pot to "sauté."
2. Pour in the stock and bay leaf. Mix.
3. In this order, add the chicken, onion, garlic, oregano, and tomatoes.
4. Select the "Poultry" setting and secure the lid.
5. After 15 minutes, the timer will beep.
6. Release the pressure by opening the valve slowly and carefully, and not all at once.
7. Open the lid and mix everything, picking out the bay leaf.
8. Plate the chicken and turn on the cooker to "sauté" again, to thicken the sauce.
9. When thick, pour over the chicken and serve with black olives on top.

Nutritional Info (⅙ recipe):

Total calories - 316
Protein - 22
Carbs - 9

Fiber - 2
Fat - 18

The Easiest Italian Chicken

Serves: 6
Time: 15-2o minutes

It's hard to go wrong with Italian, and it's hard to go wrong with chicken. When they combine, you get a tasty, easy meal that everyone in the family will love. This particular Italian chicken is made with carrots, cremini mushrooms, cherry tomatoes, and green olives. If there's an ingredient a member of your family doesn't like, just leave it out.

Ingredients:
8 boneless, skinless chicken thighs
2 medium-sized, chopped carrots
½ pound stemmed and quartered cremini mushrooms
2 cups cherry tomatoes
3 smashed garlic cloves
½ cup pitted green olives
½ cup thinly-sliced fresh basil
¼ cup chopped fresh Italian parsley
1 chopped onion
1 tablespoon olive oil
1 tablespoon tomato paste
½ teaspoon black pepper
Salt to taste

Directions:

1. Season the chicken thighs with salt.
2. On your Instant Pot, hit "sauté" and pour in the olive oil.
3. When shiny, toss in the carrots, mushrooms, onions, and a little salt.
4. Cook for about 3-5 minutes until soft.
5. Add the smashed garlic and tomato paste and cook for another 30 seconds.
6. Last, add the cherry tomatoes, chicken thighs, and olives.
7. Turn off "sauté" before locking the pressure cooker.
8. Hit "Manual," and choose 10 minutes on "high pressure."
9. When the beeper goes off, quick-release the pressure right away.
10. Take off the lid and season.
11. Plate and serve!

Nutritional Info (⅙ recipe):

Total calories - 245
Protein - 35
Carbs - 1o
Fiber - 3
Fat - 8

Salsa Verde Chicken

Serves: 6
Time: 25 minutes

I love using salsa in recipes, because it's a cheap and easy way to add a ton of flavor to whatever dish it's in. In this case, it's salsa verde, and the dish is shredded chicken. You can use the finished product in a whole bunch of ways, like in a casserole, burrito, sandwich, taco, or over lettuce.

Ingredients:

2 ½ pounds of boneless chicken breasts
16-ounces of salsa verde
1 teaspoon smoked paprika
1 teaspoon cumin
1 teaspoon salt

Directions:

1. Throw everything into your Instant Pot pressure cooker.
2. Select "Manual," and then 25 minutes at "high pressure."
3. When the timer goes off, quick-release the pressure.
4. Carefully open the cooker and shred the chicken.
5. Eat and enjoy!

Nutritional Info (⅙ recipe):

Total calories - 340
Protein - 59
Carbs - 6
Fiber - 0
Fat - 7

Simple 'n Classic Chicken Soup

Serves: 4
Time: 50 minutes

With just six ingredients, you can make a simple and delicious chicken soup that's perfect for when you're feeling under the weather. No need to buy the canned stuff anymore!

Ingredients:

16-ounces water
16-ounces chicken stock
2 frozen, boneless chicken breasts
4 medium-sized potatoes
Three peeled carrots
½ big diced onion
Salt and pepper

Directions:

1. Put everything into the pressure cooker, including salt and pepper.
2. Turn on your Instant Pot by selecting Manual, and then 35 minutes on "high pressure."
3. When time is up, turn off the cooker and wait 15 minutes for the pressure to come down by itself.
4. Carefully open the cooker, stir, and serve!

Nutritional Info (¼ recipe):

Total calories - 72
Protein - 5
Carbs - 7
Fiber - 0
Fat - 0

Chicken Tortilla Soup

Serves: 4
Time: 30 minutes

Sometimes the classic chicken noodle soup needs a bit of a kick. This zesty chicken tortilla soup is the answer. It's super easy with the Instant Pot's "Soup" setting and full of great ingredients like tomato, beans, corn, and of course, tortillas.

Ingredients:

2, 6-inch corn tortillas cut into 1-inch squares
3-4 cups chicken broth
3 chicken breasts
1 big, chopped tomato
1 chopped onion
2 minced garlic cloves
15-ounces of black beans
1 cup frozen corn
2 tablespoons chopped cilantro
1 bay leaf
1 tablespoon olive oil
2 teaspoons chili powder
1 teaspoon ground cumin
¼ teaspoon ground cayenne pepper

Directions:

1. Turn on the Instant Pot to "sauté."
2. Pour in the olive oil and cook the onion while stirring until soft.
3. Add the cilantro, garlic, and tortillas.
4. Stir and wait 1 minute.
5. Add the black beans, corn, tomato, 3 cups of broth, chicken, and spices.
6. Turn off the "sauté" function and close the lid.
7. Switch over to "Soup" mode and adjust the time to just 4 minutes.
8. When time is up, quick-release the pressure.
9. Carefully take out the chicken and shred before returning back to the pot.

10. Stir everything well.
11. Serve with cilantro, cheese, lime juice, and any other toppings you enjoy.

Nutritional Info (¼ recipe):

Total calories - 200
Protein - 7
Carbs - 24
Fiber - 2
Fat - 9

Chipotle-Chocolate Chicken Chili

Serves: 6
Time: 45 minutes

It's amazing what chocolate can do. If you've never used it in a savory way, get ready to be amazed. Chipotle and chocolate are a match made in heaven, and this chili is so good you'll want to make it your go-to for cold winter nights and as leftovers (if there are any) for lunch the next day.

Ingredients:

1 pound ground chicken
1 cup chicken broth
1 chopped onion
1 chopped red bell pepper
2-3 minced garlic cloves
Two, 14.5-ounce cans of crushed tomatoes
15-ounces rinsed and drained dark red kidney beans
2 chipotle chilis
2 tablespoons of adobo sauce (from the can of chipotle chilis)
2 tablespoons brown sugar
2 tablespoons unsweetened cocoa powder
2 tablespoons chili powder
2 teaspoons olive oil
1 teaspoon apple cider vinegar
1 teaspoon ground cumin
¼ teaspoon salt

Directions:

1. Pour olive oil into the Instant Pot and click "sauté."
2. When the oil is shiny and hot, add the onion, garlic, bell pepper, and meat.
3. Cook and stir frequently, until the veggies are soft and the meat is brown.
4. Add everything else except the vinegar and chopped chocolate bits.
5. Hit "Cancel" and close the pressure cooker lid.
6. Select "Manual" and then 10 minutes at "high pressure."
7. When the beep sounds, quick-release the pressure.

8. Open the lid and stir in chocolate and vinegar.
9. Time to eat!

Nutritional Info (⅙ recipe):

Total calories - 436
Protein - 42
Carbs - 39
Fiber - 12
Fat - 14

French Onion Chicken Thighs

Serves: 4-6
Time: 30 minutes

Do you love French onion soup? How about chicken? What about chicken that tastes like French onion soup? Chicken thighs cook in an Instant Pot with onions, wine, butter, and herbs. After everything is cooked, you add Gruyere cheese - a must for French onion soup - and dig in!

Ingredients:

8 bone-in chicken thighs
3 big, thinly-sliced yellow onions
1 cup grated Gruyere cheese
½ cup beef broth
½ cup dry white wine
1 tablespoon olive oil
1 tablespoon butter
2 teaspoons fresh thyme
½ teaspoon sugar
½ teaspoon black pepper
½ teaspoon salt

Directions:

1. Turn your Instant Pot to "Sauté" and melt the butter.
2. When shiny, add the chicken and brown on all sides, for a total of 6 minutes.
3. Move to a bowl.
4. Toss in the salt, sugar, and onions.
5. Cook for about 20 minutes.
6. Pour in the wine and deglaze the pot.
7. Add thyme, pepper, and broth.
8. Return the meat to the pot and stir everything together.
9. Secure the lid.
10. Hit "Manual," and then 18 minutes at "high pressure."
11. Hit "Cancel" and let the pressure decrease naturally.
12. Open the lid.

13. Sprinkle on cheese.
14. Close the lid so the cheese can melt, using the leftover heat.
15. Serve the chicken with sauce.

Nutritional Info (¼ recipe):

Total calories: 483
Protein: 57
Carbs: 8
Fiber: 0
Fat: 23

Herb-Braised Chicken Leg Quarters

Serves: 4-6
Time: 30 minutes

Chicken with herbs is a classic French dish, and perfect for the Instant Pot. Make sure to use fresh herbs; dried ones don't have enough flavor. For a side, go with fresh bread or a salad.

Ingredients:

3 ½ pounds of skin-on chicken leg-and-thigh quarters
1 chopped yellow onion
4 chopped celery stalks
½ cup chicken broth
½ cup dry white wine
2 tablespoons olive oil
2 teaspoons minced garlic
2 teaspoons fresh thyme
2 teaspoons minced oregano
2 teaspoons minced fresh sage
½ teaspoon salt

Directions:

1. Pour oil in the Instant Pot and heat on the "Sauté" function.
2. Season chicken with salt and pepper.
3. Brown on each side for 3 minutes, for a total of 6 minutes.
4. Toss in celery and onion, and cook for 4 minutes.
5. Add garlic.
6. Add herbs before pouring in the broth and wine.
7. Deglaze.
8. Add chicken back to the pot.
9. Secure and lock the lid.
10. Hit "Manual," and cook for 18 minutes on "high pressure."
11. When time is up, hit "Cancel" and wait for the pressure to come down naturally.
12. Open up the lid.
13. Serve chicken with sauce.

Nutritional Info (¼ recipe):

Total calories: 335
Protein: 49
Carbs: 5
Fiber: 1
Fat: 12

The Most Basic Pressure-Cooked Chicken

Serves: 8
Time: 30 minutes

Want to make the easiest whole chicken in your pressure cooker? This recipe is so basic, it doesn't even need water. You can use any seasonings you want; the ingredients here are just suggestions.

Ingredients:

1 medium-sized, whole chicken
1 minced green onion
2 tablespoons sugar
1 tablespoon cooking wine
1 minced piece of ginger
2 teaspoons soy sauce
2 teaspoons salt

Directions:

1. Season the chicken thoroughly with salt and sugar.
2. Sprinkle 1 teaspoon of salt into the bottom of the Instant Pot.
3. Pour the wine and soy sauce into the cooker, and add the chicken.
4. Choose "Poultry" and cook.
5. When time is up, flip the chicken, and push "Poultry" again.
6. Let the pressure come down naturally before opening the cooker.
7. Serve chicken pieces with green onion on top and any side dishes you'd like.

Nutritional Info (⅛ recipe):

Total calories - 131
Protein -18
Carbs - 4

Fiber - 0
Fat - 5

Chapter 7

Ethnic

Sticky Moroccan Chicken Drumsticks

Serves: 2
Time: 50 minutes

Sticky-sweet chicken drumsticks are always good, and then when you add some Moroccan spices like coriander and saffron, they're even better. You should be able to find everything at a regular grocery store, and if you can't find saffron threads, check out an Asian market.

Ingredients:

1 pound chicken drumsticks
Zest and juice of one medium lemon
¼ cup honey
2 teaspoons blackstrap molasses
1 teaspoon garlic powder
1 teaspoon paprika
1 teaspoon ground cumin
1 teaspoon sea salt
½ teaspoon ground cinnamon
½ teaspoon ground ginger
½ teaspoon black pepper
¼ teaspoon ground coriander
¼ teaspoon packed saffron threads, crushed

Directions:

1. Dry the chicken with paper towels.
2. Mix the paprika, garlic, ginger, cumin, cinnamon, coriander, saffron,

salt, and pepper to make the spice rub.
3. Coat both sides of the chicken.
4. Turn your Instant Pot to "sauté."
5. When hot, pour in some olive oil.
6. Brown the drumsticks all over.
7. Hit "Cancel" and close the pressure cooker.
8. Select "Manual" and then 10 minutes on "high pressure."
9. When time is up, hit "Cancel" and slowly release the pressure manually.
10. Take out the chicken with tongs and place in a bowl.
11. Cover with foil.
12. With the cooking juices in the cooker, turn the Instant Pot back to "sauté."
13. In a separate bowl, mix lemon zest, lemon juice, honey, and molasses.
14. Add to cooker.
15. Bring to a rolling boil, whisking, until reduced and thick.
16. With tongs, roll the drumsticks in the sauce and plate.
17. Garnish with chopped scallions and serve!

Nutritional Info (½ recipe):

Total calories - 300
Protein - 22
Carbs - 34
Fiber - 1
Fat - 10

Thai Lime Chicken

Serves: 4
Time: 15 minutes

This simple chicken recipe is perfect for summer. Fresh, bright flavors from the chopped mint, lime juice, and fish sauce keep the chicken light and refreshing, even on the hottest days of the summer. You can find coconut nectar on Amazon or stores like Walmart.

Ingredients:

2 pounds boneless, skinless chicken thighs
1 cup lime juice
½ cup fish sauce (like Red Boat)
¼ cup olive oil
2 tablespoons coconut nectar
2 teaspoons chopped cilantro
1 teaspoon chopped mint
1 teaspoon grated ginger

Directions:

1. Put the thighs in the bottom of your Instant Pot.
2. Mix everything in a bowl and pour over the chicken.
3. Hit "Poultry" and then "-" button to 10 minutes.
4. When time is up, quick-release the pressure.
5. Drain any extra liquid and serve!

Nutritional Info (¼ recipe):

Total calories - 518
Protein - 36
Carbs - 13
Fiber - 0
Fat - 36

Lamb, Date, + Walnut Stew

Serves: 4
Time: 50 minutes

This stew is like a tajine, which is an Arabian and North-African slow-cooked stew with spices like ginger and cinnamon. This recipe uses lamb, which is also common in a tajine, as well as dried dates and walnuts. The result is a delicious meal that's much more interesting than the usual beef-and-potatoes stew.

Ingredients:

2 ½ pounds boneless leg of lamb
1 thinly-sliced red onion
1 cup pitted dried dates, cut in half
½ cup chicken broth
½ cup walnuts
½ cup unsweetened apple juice
2 tablespoons olive oil
½ tablespoon ground cinnamon
1 teaspoon ground ginger
½ teaspoon salt
¼ teaspoon grated nutmeg
¼ teaspoon allspice

Directions:

1. Mix ginger, cinnamon, allspice, nutmeg, and salt in a bowl.
2. Coat the lamb in the spices.
3. Turn your Instant Pot to "Sauté" and heat the olive oil.
4. When shiny, add the onion and soften for 5 minutes.
5. Add the meat into the pot and brown.
6. Toss in the dates, walnuts, apple juice, and broth, and deglaze.
7. Close and lock the lid.
8. Press "Manual," and then 38 minutes on "high pressure."
9. When the timer goes off, hit "Cancel" and let the pressure go down naturally.
10. Open the lid and stir.
11. Serve!

Nutritional Info (¼ recipe):

Total calories: 897
Protein: 76
Carbs: 23
Fiber: 1
Fat: 57

North African Osso Buco

Serves: 4
Time: 1 hour, 20 minutes (+ four hours marinade time)

Osso Buco is traditionally an Italian dish, but by changing out some spices, you get a dish that's more reminiscent of what you find in North Africa. By marinating the veal in a paste made from oil, garlic, and lemon zest, you start off with an already-flavorful dish. Add in other ingredients like ginger, turmeric, allspice, tomato, and white wine, and you'll want to lick your plate.

Ingredients:

4 pounds of veal shank (four separate shanks)
1 big onion, sliced very thin
1 cup white wine
14-ounce can of diced tomatoes
1 medium-sized lemon, cut into quarters
2 tablespoons minced garlic
2 tablespoons butter
2 tablespoons olive oil
2 tablespoons grated lemon zest
One, 4-inch cinnamon stick
½ teaspoon ground ginger
½ teaspoon salt
½ teaspoon ground allspice
½ teaspoon ground cardamom
½ teaspoon ground turmeric
½ teaspoon grated nutmeg

Directions:

1. In a bowl, mix oil, garlic, salt, and olive oil.
2. Rub all over the meat.
3. Plate meat, cover with plastic wrap, and store in fridge for at least 4 hours.
4. In your Instant Pot, melt the butter on "Sauté."
5. Add veal in batches and brown for about 8 minutes.
6. Add the onion and soften for 4 minutes.

7. Toss in the ginger, cardamom, allspice, turmeric, and nutmeg.
8. Cook until the spices become fragrant.
9. Pour in the wine and deglaze, letting it come to a boil.
10. Return the meat to the pot, along with the tomatoes.
11. Toss in the cinnamon stick and quartered lemon.
12. Secure the lid.
13. Hit "Manual," and then select "high pressure" for 50 minutes.
14. When time is up, hit "Cancel" and wait for a natural-pressure release.
15. Open the pot.
16. Pick out the cinnamon stick before serving.

Nutritional Info (¼ recipe):

Total calories - 444
Protein - 73
Carbs - 11
Fiber - 2.8
Fat - 10

Roasted Red Pepper + Eggplant Dip

Serves: 6-8
Time: 2o minutes

A take on the Middle Eastern Baba Ganoush, this roasted red pepper and eggplant dip is a little less smoky, but still goes great with the traditional pita bread. It's a great alternative to unhealthy, fatty chip-dips.

Ingredients:

2 pounds eggplant cut into 1-inch chunks
4 minced garlic cloves
¼ chopped roasted red peppers
5 tablespoons olive oil
1 cup water
5 tablespoons lemon juice
1 tablespoon tahini
1 tablespoon cumin
1 teaspoon salt
Black pepper

Directions:

1. Turn your Instant Pot to "Sauté."
2. Pour in 3 tablespoons of olive oil.
3. Add half of the eggplant and brown on one side for about 4 minutes.
4. Take out the eggplant and pour in another tablespoon of oil.
5. Add garlic and the rest of the unbrowned eggplant.
6. Cook 1 minute before adding the browned eggplant back into the pot, along with water and salt.
7. Close and lock the lid.
8. Press "Manual" and 3 minutes on "high pressure."
9. When the timer goes off, hit "Cancel" and quick-release.
10. Add red peppers, stir, and let them warm up.
11. After 5 minutes, drain the cooking liquid.
12. Add the lemon juice, 1 tablespoon of oil, tahini, black pepper, and cumin.
13. Using a blender or food processor, puree till creamy.

14. Serve with pita or chips.

Nutritional Info:

Total calories - 165
Protein - 3
Carbs - 12
Fiber - 6
Fat - 2

Quinoa Tabbouleh

Serves: 4-6
Time: 20 minutes

For this recipe, you swap out the traditional bulgur wheat for quinoa, which is higher in protein and gluten-free. Fresh tomato, cucumber, lemon, and mint brighten up the fluffy quinoa, and if you add spinach, you have a satisfying meal-salad!

Ingredients:

1 ⅔ cups water
1 cup rinsed and drained quinoa
1 chopped tomato
1 chopped cucumber

Juice of 1 lemon
1 minced garlic clove
½ cup chopped mint
2 tablespoons olive oil
Salt + pepper

Directions:

1. Pour water, quinoa, 1 tablespoon of oil, and salt into the Instant Pot.
2. Close the lid.
3. Press "Manual" and 1 minute on "high pressure."
4. When time is up, hit "Cancel" and wait for pressure to release naturally.
5. Move the quinoa to a bowl to cool.
6. Mix in the cucumber, tomato, garlic, mint, lemon juice, and 1 tablespoon of oil.
7. Season to taste with salt and pepper.
8. Serve!

Nutritional Info:

Total calories - 256
Protein - 8
Carbs - 35

Fiber - 4
Fat – 1

Instant Pot Hummus

Serves: 8-10
Time: 1 hour, 10 minutes

4 cups water
8 ounces rinsed and dried chickpeas
3 minced garlic cloves
6 tablespoons olive oil
⅓ cup tahini
¼ cup lemon juice
1 ½ teaspoons salt
½ teaspoon smoked paprika

Directions:

1. Add water, chickpeas, and 2 tablespoons of olive oil to the Instant Pot.
2. Close and lock the lid.
3. Hit "Manual" and select "high pressure" for 45 minutes.
4. When time is up, hit "Cancel" and wait for the pressure to decrease naturally.
5. The chickpeas should be soft, but not mushy.
6. Drain the chickpeas, saving one cup of cooking liquid.
7. Put the chickpeas in a food processor and puree with 4 tablespoons of olive oil, salt, garlic, lemon juice, paprika, and ¼ cup of cooking liquid.
8. Add additional liquid to get the texture you want.
9. The hummus will last up to five days covered in the fridge.

Nutritional Info:

Total calories - 264
Protein - 8
Carbs - 20

Fiber - 6
Fat - 3

Chinese Pork Belly

Serves: 4
Time: About 40 minutes

This recipe is a traditional Chinese dish and uses ingredients like star anise, garlic, and ginger. Star anise is a spice from Vietnam and China, and can be found at any Asian market. While you're there, pick up some Chinese cooking wine.

Ingredients:

2 pounds of pork belly sliced into 5-inch pieces
2 cups water
½ cup soy sauce
6 sliced garlic cloves
5 slices fresh ginger
4 star anise

3 tablespoons Chinese cooking wine
2 teaspoons cane sugar
1 teaspoon ground white pepper

Directions:

1. Turn on your Instant Pot to "sauté" and add a little oil.
2. When shiny, sear the pork belly slices on both sides, which should take about 2 minutes per side.
3. Throw in the garlic and ginger.
4. Cook and stir for another 5 minutes.
5. Add in the rest of the ingredients and lock the pressure cooker.
6. Select "Manual," and then cook for 30 minutes.
7. Press "Cancel" and quick-release the pressure when the timer goes off.
8. The pork belly should be extremely tender.
9. Serve with rice and veggies.

Nutritional Info (¼ recipe):

Total calories - 365
Protein - 24.5
Carbs - 7

Fiber - 0
Fat - 30

Mango Dal

Serves: 4-6
Time: About 50 minutes

A classic Indian ingredient, mango and chana dal are the stars of this dish. Chana dal is a kind of chickpea with an earthy, sweet flavor. Bob's Red Mill sells dal, so it shouldn't be too hard to find. In addition to the mango, the beans are mixed with onion, garlic, and lots of Indian spices like turmeric and cumin. You can easily make this vegetarian (substitute chicken broth with veggie broth) or add grilled chicken for a heartier meal.

Ingredients:

4 cups chicken broth
1 cup chana dal
2 peeled and diced mangoes
4 minced garlic cloves
½ cup chopped cilantro
1 minced onion
1 tablespoon minced ginger
1 tablespoon coconut oil
Juice from ½ lime
1 teaspoon ground cumin
1 teaspoon sea salt
1 teaspoon ground coriander
1 teaspoon ground turmeric
⅛ teaspoon cayenne pepper

Directions:

1. Rinse the dal in a colander.
2. Turn the Instant Pot to "sauté" and heat coconut oil.
3. Add the cumin and cook for about 30 seconds.
4. Toss in the onion and cook for 5 minutes, until soft.
5. Next, add the coriander, ginger, cayenne, garlic, and salt.
6. Pour in the broth and add the dal and turmeric.
7. Keep the pot on "sauté" and bring the contents to a boil.
8. It should boil for about 10 minutes. If it gets foamy, skim it off with a large spoon.
9. Add the mangoes.
10. Secure the lid and hit "Beans/Chili," and then 20 minutes.

11. When time is up, hit "Cancel" and wait for the pressure to reduce naturally.
12. Add the lime juice and cilantro.
13. Serve with rice.

Nutritional Info (¼ recipe):

Total calories - 486
Protein - 21
Carbs - 91
Fiber - 11
Fat - 3

Easy Filipino Chicken Adobo

Serves: 5-6
Time: About 15 minutes

There aren't any unusual ingredients in this recipe, so a big shopping trip isn't necessary. If you're planning on using Nishiki white rice, just stop by any Asian market or buy some from Amazon. Filipino adobo is not like Spanish adobo, so don't use a pre-made adobo spice. Just soy sauce, garlic, white vinegar, and the other seasonings are needed.

Ingredients:

4-5 pounds of chicken thighs
4 crushed garlic cloves
3 bay leaves
½ cup soy sauce
½ cup white vinegar
1 teaspoon black peppercorns

Directions:

1. Throw everything in the pressure cooker and secure the lid.
2. Hit "Poultry" and adjust to 15 minutes.
3. When ready, quick-release.
4. Serve with Nishiki white rice.

Nutritional Info (⅕ recipe):

Total calories - 526
Protein - 90
Carbs - 9
Fiber - 0
Fat - 14

Chicken Curry

Serves: 6
Time: 15 minutes + 1 hour marinade

Chicken curry is an Indian classic and can't be beat flavor-wise. Pressure cookers are extremely popular in India, so you know any recipe from that area is going to be great. You'll definitely want to stock up on spices like garam masala, turmeric, and coriander seeds, and make curries a regular meal.

Ingredients:

6 boneless chicken breasts
2 tablespoons olive oil
1 chopped tomato
1 yellow onion
2 teaspoons garam masala powder
1 teaspoon grated ginger
1 teaspoon chili powder
1 teaspoon coriander seeds
Salt

Juice of 1 lemon
2 teaspoons ginger powder
2 teaspoons coriander powder
2 teaspoons garlic powder
1 ¼ teaspoons chili powder
½ teaspoon turmeric
Salt

Directions:

1. Mix the ingredients in the second list and rub over the chicken.
2. Place in a bag and chill in the fridge for an hour.
3. When ready, heat oil in the Instant Pot on "sauté."
4. Toss in the coriander seeds and heat them till a few pop open.
5. Add the chopped onion and cook till they become clear.
6. Add in the garam masala, coriander powder, chili powder, garlic, and ginger.

7. After a few minutes, add chopped tomatoes until they soften.
8. Take out the chicken and sauté to brown them a little.
9. Close the pot lid.
10. Choose "Poultry" and adjust to 8 minutes on "high pressure."
11. When ready, quick-release the pressure.
12. Serve with the tomatoes and onions, and rice.

Nutritional Info (⅙ recipe):

Total calories - 234
Protein - 19.9
Carbs - 9.7
Fiber - 3
Fat - 12.7

Chickpea Curry

Serves: 3-4
Time: About 35 minutes + overnight soak

If you're a vegetarian and at a loss about meals, look to India. The religions of Hindu and Jain are associated with vegetarianism, so there's a long tradition of non-meat cuisine. This curry is chickpea-based and bolstered with tomatoes, onions, and lots of spices.

Ingredients:

2 cups dry chickpeas
1 can diced tomatoes
1 big, diced onion
4-6 tablespoons olive oil
2 tablespoons chholey masala
2-4 tablespoons lemon juice
1 tablespoon garlic paste
1 tablespoon ginger paste
1 teaspoon turmeric
½ teaspoon garam masala
Coriander leaves
Salt

Directions:

1. Soak the chickpeas in water in a bowl on the counter overnight.
2. The next day, pour 2 cups of water into your Instant Pot and hit "sauté."
3. When the water is boiling, add chickpeas.
4. Boil for 10 minutes.
5. When time is up, pour the peas and water into another bowl.
6. Heat oil in the pot.
7. Add garam masala and diced onion.
8. When clear, add turmeric.
9. Toss in ginger and garlic paste, and stir.
10. Add tomatoes and cook for a few minutes.
11. Add chholey masala.
12. Pour in chickpeas with their water.

13. Sprinkle in a little salt.
14. Close and secure the lid.
15. Hit "Manual" and then adjust to 20 minutes on "high pressure."
16. When the timer beeps, hit "Cancel" and wait for the pressure to reduce naturally.
17. Add coriander leaves and lemon juice before serving.

Nutritional Info (¼ recipe):

Total calories - 177
Protein - 5.9
Carbs - 29
Fiber - 6.2
Fat -5

Arroz con Pollo

Serves: 6-8
Time: About 40 minutes (+ one hour soak time)

"Arroz con Pollo" literally means "chicken rice." The chicken of choice are thighs that have been marinated in oil, garlic, lime, cumin, and oregano. The rice is brown, and cooked with Spanish olives, tomatoes, onion, and seasonings. There's also a sofrito, which is just a basic Spanish sauce made from tomatoes, peppers, and garlic. You only use the Instant Pot to cook everything and have a hearty meal for 6-8 people in less than an hour.

Ingredients:

12 boneless, skinless chicken thighs
3 chopped garlic cloves
¼ cup olive oil
3 tablespoons minced oregano
2 tablespoons lime juice
1 tablespoon salt
2 teaspoons cumin
½ teaspoon black pepper
3 garlic cloves
½ seeded and chopped green bell pepper
½ chopped yellow onion
1 bunch of cilantro
½ teaspoon salt
¼ teaspoon black pepper

5 cups chicken stock
3 cups long-grain brown rice
28-ounces of fire-roasted, diced tomatoes (with liquid)
1 ½ cups Spanish olives
1 seeded and diced bell pepper
2 tablespoons olive brine
2 tablespoons coconut oil
1 tablespoon minced oregano
1 teaspoon ground cumin
¼ teaspoon salt

Directions:

1. Mix the ingredients in the first list and coat the chicken with it. This should marinate for at least 1 hour.
2. To make the sofrito, mix the ingredients in the second list in a food processor till smooth.
3. Turn your pressure cooker to "sauté" and melt the coconut oil.
4. Take out the chicken and brown, 5 minutes on each side.
5. Plate.
6. Toss in the onion, red bell pepper, cumin, and oregano (from the last ingredient list) into the pot and sauté till tender.
7. Stir in the sofrito and cook for 3 minutes.
8. Add the diced tomatoes, salt, and stock, and let everything simmer for 2 minutes.
9. Add the olives, olive brine, and rice.
10. Lastly, return the chicken to the Instant Pot.
11. Lock the lid.
12. Hit "Meat/Stew" and adjust time to 15 minutes.
13. When the beeper goes off, hit "Cancel" and wait for the pressure to come down on its own.
14. Serve!

Nutritional Info (⅙ recipe):

Total calories - 257
Protein - 13
Carbs - 28
Fiber - 1
Fat - 10

Coconut Chicken Curry

Serves: 6
Time: About 45-50 minutes

What makes this particular curry unique is the use of whole spices, like cinnamon sticks and cardamom pods. Whole spices are fresher and last longer, and you can get big bags of them at Asian markets.

Ingredients:

6 peeled and halved shallots
4 whole cloves
4 little dried red chilies
3 green cardamom pods
¾ cup grated, unsweetened coconut
1-inch cinnamon stick
2 teaspoons black peppercorns
2 teaspoons fennel seeds
2 teaspoons coriander seeds
1 teaspoon cumin seeds
1 teaspoon brown mustard seeds
1 teaspoon turmeric powder

3 pounds boneless, skinless chicken thighs (cut into pieces)
1 tablespoon coconut oil
2 minced garlic cloves
2 sliced tomatoes
2 sliced yellow onions
1 inch minced ginger
1 tablespoon vinegar
3 teaspoons salt

Directions:

1. We'll tackle the first ingredient list right away. Turn on the Instant Pot to "Sauté."
2. Throw in the chiles and shallots, and roast until parts have blackened.
3. Carefully take them out with tongs and put them in a food

processor bowl. Do not blend yet.

4. Add the shredded coconut and whole spices to the Instant Pot and stir for 1 minute. The coconut should be a pale brown, and the spices fragrant and toasty.
5. Add the turmeric and stir for a few more seconds before moving everything to the food processor.
6. Pulse with 4-6 tablespoons of water until you get a paste.
7. Keep the paste in the bowl for now.
8. Return to the pressure cooker and add oil.
9. When shiny and hot, add the ginger, onions, and garlic.
10. Cook for 10-15 minutes until onions have softened and browned.
11. Add the coconut paste and cook for 1 minute.
12. Throw in the tomatoes and cook for 5 minutes.
13. Lastly, add the vinegar, salt, and chicken.
14. Stir everything before locking the pressure cooker lid.
15. Hit "Manual," and then adjust to 10 minutes on "high pressure."
16. When time is up, hit "Cancel" and wait for the pressure to come down.
17. Serve with plain yogurt and rice.

Nutritional Info (⅙ recipe):

Total calories - 320
Protein - 47
Carbs - 5
Fiber - 4
Fat - 9

69

Spicy Mahi-Mahi w/ Honey + Orange

Serves: 2
Time: About 5-6 minutes

Mahi-mahi is a beautifully flaky, white fish with a mild taste. On its own, it's a bit bland, but this recipe spices things up with sriracha, lime, ginger, honey, and sweet orange juice. You also use Nanami Togarashi, the Asian spice mix, which you can find on Amazon or Asian markets. All in all, this is a lightning-fast, lip-smacking meal with not that many ingredients you can make on any day of the week.

Ingredients:

2 mahi-mahi fillets
2 tablespoons sriracha
2 tablespoons honey
Juice of ½ lime
2 minced garlic cloves
1-inch grated ginger piece
1 tablespoon Nanami Togarashi
1 tablespoon Simply Orange Mango juice
Salt
Pepper

Directions:

1. Season fish with salt and pepper.
2. In a bowl, mix honey, sriracha, OJ, lime juice, and Nanami Togarashi.
3. Pour 1 cup of water into the Instant Pot.
4. Lower in the steam rack and put the fillets inside.
5. Pour sauce on top of fish.
6. Secure the Instant Pot lid.
7. Hit "Manual" and adjust time to 5 minutes.
8. When the beeper goes off, quick-release the pressure.
9. Open the lid and serve with a side dish like rice pilaf or veggies.

Nutritional Info (½ recipe):

Total calories - 229
Protein - 32
Carbs - 23
Fiber - 0
Fat - 1

Pork Fried Rice

Serves: 4
Time: 40 minutes

Skip the takeout and make this classic yourself. It's a fast, tasty meal that's perfect for lunch leftovers the next day. I've included it in the "Ethnic" section because it's typically at Chinese restaurants, but there's nothing unusual in the ingredients' list.

Ingredients:

3 cups + 2 tablespoons water
2 cups white rice
8-ounces thin pork loin, cut into ½-inch slices
1 beaten egg
½ cup frozen peas
1 chopped onion
1 peeled and chopped carrot
3 tablespoons olive oil
3 tablespoons soy sauce
Salt + pepper

Directions:

1. Turn your Instant Pot to "Sauté."
2. Pour in 1 tablespoon of oil and cook the carrot and onion for 2 minutes.
3. Season the pork.
4. Cook in the pot for 5 minutes.
5. Hit "Cancel" and take out the onion, carrot, and pork.
6. Deglaze with the water.
7. Add rice and a bit of salt.
8. Lock the lid.
9. Hit "Rice" and cook for the default time.
10. When time is up, hit "Cancel" and wait 10 minutes.
11. Release any leftover steam.
12. Stir the rice, making a hollow in the middle so you can see the bottom of the pot.
13. Hit "Sauté" and add 2 tablespoons of oil.

14. Add the egg in the hollow and whisk it around to scramble it while it cooks.
15. When cooked, pour in peas, onion, carrot, and pork.
16. Stir until everything has warmed together.
17. Stir in soy sauce, hit "Cancel," and serve.

Nutritional Info (¼ recipe):

Total calories - 547
Protein - 22
Carbs - 81
Fiber - 3
Fat - 2

Hawaiian Pork

Serves: 8
Time: 2 hours

Hawaiian pork is usually cooked extremely slowly. Imagine a luau where a whole pig is slow-roasted over a fire. The result is melt-in-your-mouth tender. You can get similar results in an Instant Pot, just faster!

Ingredients:

5 pounds bone-in pork roast
6 minced garlic cloves
1 cup water
1 quartered onion
1 ½ tablespoons red Hawaiian coarse salt
Black pepper

Directions:

1. Cut the meat into 3 pieces.
2. Put in the Instant Pot.
3. Add in garlic, onion, and salt.
4. Season with black pepper.
5. Pour in the water and lock the lid.
6. Hit "Manual," and cook for 1 ½ hours on "high pressure."
7. When time is done, hit "Cancel," and wait for the pressure to decrease naturally.
8. Before serving, shred the pork with two forks.

Nutritional Info (⅛ recipe):

Total calories - 536
Protein - 51
Carbs - 2
Fiber - 0
Fat - 13

Chapter 8

Beef

Spicy Barbacoa

Serves: 4
Time: About 1 hour, 15 minutes

Barbacoa originally came from the Caribbean and became popular in Mexico. It's where the word "barbecue" comes from. It refers to any kind of meat that's slow-cooked over an open fire, but in an Instant Pot, it cooks much faster. This recipe is for beef seasoned with ingredients like chipotle peppers, lime juice, cumin, and so on.

Ingredients:

2-3 pounds beef chuck roast
3 bay leaves
3 chipotle peppers + 1 tablespoon adobo sauce from can
1 cup beef broth
Juice of ½ lime
⅓ cup apple cider vinegar
2 tablespoons cooking fat
1 ½ tablespoons ground cumin
1 ½ tablespoons salt
1 tablespoon black pepper
1 tablespoon tomato paste
2 teaspoons oregano
1 teaspoon onion powder
1 teaspoon cinnamon
¼ teaspoon ground cloves

<u>Directions:</u>

1. Turn your pot to "Sauté."
2. Trim the beef and dry with a paper towel.
3. Season with ½ tablespoon salt and ½ tablespoon of pepper.
4. Put the fat in the pot and melt.
5. Add beef and sear all over.
6. In a blender, mix vinegar, peppers, adobo, lime juice, cumin, salt, pepper, tomato paste, onion powder, cloves, oregano, and cinnamon until smooth.
7. Pour the puree in the pot so the meat is covered.
8. Toss in the bay leaves and pour in broth.
9. Secure the lid and press "Manual," and then 50 minutes on "high pressure."
10. When time is up, press "Cancel" and wait for the pressure to come down naturally.
11. When the pressure is gone, open the pot and shred the meat.
12. Serve with the cooking liquid as a sauce.

Nutritional Info:

Total calories - 165
Protein - 24
Carbs - 2
Fiber - 1
Fat - 7

Beef + Tortilla Casserole

Serves: 6
Time: About 45 minutes

This recipe takes everything you know and love about burritos, and turns them into an easy casserole. There's beef, cheese, chiles, tortillas, and spices. Everything goes in the Instant Pot for about a half hour, you release the pressure naturally, and there you go.

Ingredients:

1 ¼ pounds lean ground beef
6 corn tortillas
14-ounces of crushed tomatoes
4 ½-ounces of mild green chiles (save the liquid!)
1 chopped yellow onion
2 cups shredded Cheddar
¼ cup chopped cilantro
2 tablespoons olive oil
1 ½ tablespoons chili powder
1 tablespoon minced garlic
½ teaspoon ground cumin

Directions:

1. Turn your Instant Pot to "Sauté" and add oil.
2. Add onion and cook for 3 minutes or until soft.
3. Add chiles and garlic.
4. After 1 minute, add in the beef and brown.
5. After 4 minutes, add chili powder and cumin.
6. Quickly add the cilantro and tomatoes.
7. Stir and cook for 2 minutes.
8. Carefully pour out the beef mixture into a bowl.
9. Wash out the pot and dry.
10. Pour in 2 cups of water and lower in a trivet.
11. Find a 2-quart baking dish that will fit in the Instant Pot.
12. Layer ½ cup of the beef mixture in the dish, then one corn tortilla, followed by more sauce and ½ cup of cheese.
13. Keep going until the ingredients are gone.

14. Wrap the dish in parchment paper, and then foil.
15. Lower into the Instant Pot.
16. Hit "Manual," and then 30 minutes on "high pressure."
17. When time is up, press "Cancel" and wait for the pressure to come down naturally.
18. Open the lid.
19. Take out the dish, unwrap it, and let it cool before serving.

Nutritional Info (⅙ recipe):

Total calories - 447
Protein - 27
Carbs - 27.9
Fiber - 4
Fat - 24.3

Flank Steak w/ Sweet Potato Gravy

Serves: 4
Time: 1 hour, 10 minutes

Tender steak is paired with a sweet and spicy sweet potato gravy that includes yellow onion, thyme, sweet paprika, and ground cloves. It's an earthy, stew-like meal that's perfect for cold nights.

Ingredients:

2 pounds flank steak, cut into four pieces
1 pound peeled and grated sweet potatoes
1 cup beef broth
1 chopped yellow onion
3 tablespoons tomato paste

1 tablespoon butter
1 tablespoon olive oil
1 tablespoon sweet paprika
2 teaspoons fresh thyme
½ teaspoon salt
¼ teaspoon cayenne
¼ teaspoon ground cloves

Directions:

1. Turn your Instant Pot to "Sauté" and melt the butter.
2. Add beef and brown. You probably have to brown the meat in two batches.
3. When all the meat is browned, move to a bowl.
4. Add onion and soften for 3 minutes.
5. Throw in the sweet potato, cloves, thyme, salt, and cayenne.
6. Cook for 1 minute before pouring in the broth.
7. Stir in the tomato paste and let the mixture simmer.
8. Add the meat back into the pot.
9. Secure the lid.
10. Press "Manual," and then "high pressure" for 60 minutes.
11. When time is up, hit "Cancel" and wait for the pressure to come down naturally.
12. To serve, spoon up meat, veggies, and sauce into a bowl.

Nutritional Info (¼ recipe):

Total calories - 594
Protein - 67
Carbs - 28

Fiber - 4
Fat - 22

Beef Brisket w/ Veggies

Serves: 5
Time: About 1 hour

The classic beef brisket can take *hours* of slow-cooking, but in an Instant Pot, enough brisket for a family of 4-5 is done in just about *one* hour. You don't have to plan so far ahead, and an assortment of hearty veggies like potatoes and carrots cook right with the brisket for even more convenience.

Ingredients:

2 pounds brisket
2 ½ cups beef broth
5-6 red potatoes
4 bay leaves
2 cups carrots cut into chunks
2 chopped celery stalks
1 big yellow onion
3 tablespoons Worcestershire sauce
3 tablespoons chopped garlic
2 tablespoons olive oil
Black pepper
Knorr Demi-Glace sauce to taste

Directions:

1. Turn on the Instant Pot to the "sauté" setting.
2. Pour in 1 tablespoon of oil and onion.
3. Caramelize .
4. When ready, move to a bowl.
5. Season brisket on both sides with black pepper.
6. Pour in another tablespoon of oil into pot and sear brisket all over.
7. Close the lid.
8. Select "Manual" and then 50 minutes on "high pressure."
9. In the meantime, prepare the veggies.
10. When the meat is done, hit "Cancel" and quick-release the pressure.
11. Carefully take off the lid and add all the veggies.
12. Select "Manual" again and 10 minutes on "high pressure."
13. When the beeper sounds, hit "Cancel" and quick-release again.

14. Take out the meat and veggies, leaving the cooking liquid in the pot. Pick out the bay leaves.
15. Turn on "sauté" and bring to a boil.
16. Add about 1 tablespoon of Demi-Glace and whisk in.
17. Serve!

Nutritional Info (⅕ recipe):

Total calories - 400
Protein - 28
Carbs - 10
Fiber - 1
Fat - 18

Sweet-Spicy Meatloaf

Serves: 4
Time: About 50 minutes

Meatloaf is a classic comfort food. To make things interesting, this recipe has a sweet and spicy glaze with brown sugar and spicy brown mustard. There's very little work involved, and essentially no clean-up, either!

Ingredients:

1 pound lean ground beef
⅔ cup bread crumbs
⅔ cup diced onion
6 sliced black olives
1 egg white
2 tablespoons ketchup
2 fresh, chopped basil leaves
1 teaspoon minced garlic

½ teaspoon salt
Black pepper

¼ cup ketchup
1 tablespoon brown sugar
1 tablespoon spicy brown mustard

Directions:

1. Prepare a round, one-quart dish with a bit of olive oil.
2. Mix everything in the first ingredient list and form a loaf in the dish.
3. In a separate bowl, mix the brown sugar, ketchup, and spicy brown mustard together.
4. Brush on top of the meatloaf.
5. Cover the dish tightly with foil.
6. Pour one cup of water into the pressure cooker and lower in the trivet.
7. Place the meatloaf dish on top and close the Instant Pot lid.
8. Select "Meat/Stew," and then 45 minutes.
9. When the beep sounds, quick-release.
10. Carefully take out the hot dish.
11. Holding the meat in place, pour out any excess liquid.
12. Rest the meat before serving.

Nutritional Info (¼ recipe):

Total calories - 261
Protein - 25
Carbs - 19.2
Fiber - 0
Fat - 7.5

Instant Pot Roast

Serves: 8
Time: About 50 minutes

This pot roast supper is enough to serve 8, which makes it a great option for a dinner party where you want to serve something easy, hearty, and satisfying.

Ingredients:

4 pounds bottom roast cut into cubes
1 cup beef broth
5 minced garlic cloves
1 peeled and chopped Granny Smith apple

1 thumb of grated ginger
½ cup soy sauce
Juice of one big orange
2 tablespoons olive oil
Salt and pepper to taste

Directions:

1. Season the roast with salt and pepper.
2. Turn on your Instant Pot to "sauté."
3. When hot, pour in the olive oil and brown the roast all over.
4. Move the meat to a plate.
5. Pour in the beef broth and scrape any stuck bits of meat.
6. Pour in soy sauce and stir.
7. Put the roast back into the pot.
8. Arrange the cut apple, garlic, and ginger on top.
9. Pour in the orange juice.
10. Close the pressure cooker lid.
11. Select "Manual" and then 45 minutes on "high pressure."
12. Hit "Cancel" and quick-release the pressure when the timer beeps.
13. Serve!

Nutritional Info (⅛ recipe):

Total calories - 492
Protein - 46
Carbs - 3

Fiber - 0
Fat - 37

Teriyaki Short Ribs

Serves: 4
Time: About 45 minutes

These lip-smacking beef short ribs are packed with umami flavor from ginger, brown sugar, soy sauce, orange, and sesame oil. The beef is marinated for *at least* 4 hours, though you can go a full 24 for a really full flavor. You can serve with rice or a favorite veggie as a side.

Ingredients:

4 big beef short ribs
1 cup water
¾ cup soy sauce
1 big, halved orange
½ cup brown sugar
1 full garlic bulb, peeled and crushed
1 large thumb of peeled and crushed fresh ginger
½ tablespoon sesame oil
Dried pepper flakes
A bunch of chopped green onions

Directions:

1. In a Ziploc bag, mix water, sugar, and soy sauce.
2. Squish around until the sugar has dissolved.
3. Add the orange juice and stir, before adding the orange slices as well.
4. Lastly, throw in the garlic, ginger, onions, and dried pepper flakes.
5. Stir before adding the ribs.
6. Stir one last time and marinate in the fridge for at least 4 hours.
7. When ready to cook the ribs, coat the bottom of the Instant Pot with olive oil and heat.
8. Remove the ribs from the bag (save the liquid!) with tongs and quickly sear for 2-3 minutes on both sides.
9. Pour in the marinade and close the lid.
10. Select the "Meat/Stew" setting and select 30 minutes.
11. When time is up, hit "Cancel" and quick-release the pressure.
12. Serve!

Nutritional Info (¼ recipe):

Total calories - 603
Protein - 43
Carbs – 76
Fiber - 1
Fat - 10

Beefy Lasagna

Serves: 6
Time: About 30 minutes

This is lasagna as you know and love it - lots of beef, cheese, and delicious ricotta filling. You don't even have to boil the noodles beforehand, just get the oven-ready no-boil variety. With an Instant Pot, lasagna becomes a 30-minute meal!

Ingredients:

2 pounds ricotta cheese
1 pound of ground beef
24-ounces pasta sauce
8-ounces of no-boil lasagna noodles
1 package shredded mozzarella cheese
2 big eggs
¼ cup water
⅓ cup grated Parmesan
1 diced onion
1 tablespoon olive oil
2 teaspoons minced garlic
1 teaspoon Italian seasoning
Salt and pepper to taste

Directions:

1. Pour olive oil in your Instant Pot and heat until it starts to smoke.
2. Quickly add the ground beef, onions, salt, and pepper.
3. When the meat is brown and onions clear, pour in the water and pasta sauce.
4. Stir before pouring out into a bowl.
5. In a separate bowl, mix the ricotta, garlic, Italian seasoning, eggs, Parmesan, salt, and pepper together.
6. Fill the pressure cooker with ¼ inch of water.
7. Layer ⅕ of the beef mixture into the bottom before adding the noodles.
8. Pour in ⅓ of the ricotta mixture, and then more beef sauce.

9. Top with noodles, and keep going until you've used everything. The last layer should be beef sauce.
10. Close the Instant Pot lid.
11. Select "Manual," and then 7 minutes on "high pressure."
12. When the beep sounds, hit "Cancel" and quick-release the pressure.
13. Open the lid and sprinkle on the mozzarella.
14. Cool for a few minutes before serving.

Nutritional Info (⅙ recipe):

Total calories - 408
Protein - 25.1
Carbs - 27.4
Fiber - 2.6
Fat - 22.1

Corned Beef + Cabbage in Spiced Cider

Serves: 6
Time: 1 hour, 30 minutes

Corned beef is usually just boiled in water, but this recipe uses apple cider infused with cloves and cinnamon. It makes for a much tastier meat. The cabbage and carrot cook in that broth as well, so the whole meal is flavorful and tender.

Ingredients:

3 ½ pounds rinsed corned beef
1 ½ cups unsweetened apple cider
8 whole cloves
6 big carrots, cut in half widthwise
One, 4-inch cinnamon stick
1 big cored green cabbage, cut into 6 wedges
¼ cup honey mustard

Directions:

1. Pour cider and put the cloves and cinnamon stick into the Instant Pot.
2. Lower in the steamer basket.
3. Put the corned beef on top.
4. Rub honey mustard on top.
5. Lock the lid.
6. Select "Manual," and then "high pressure" for 80 minutes.
7. When time is up, hit "Cancel" and wait for the pressure to come down by itself.
8. Open the lid and move the meat to a cutting board.
9. Take out the rack as well as the cloves and cinnamon stick.
10. Put the carrots and cabbage into the pot.
11. Lock the lid.
12. Hit "Manual," and then "high pressure" for just 8 minutes.
13. When time is up, press "Cancel" and quick-release.
14. Carve the meat into slices.
15. Serve in bowls with the meat, cabbage, carrots, and broth.

Nutritional Info (⅙ recipe):

Total calories: 473
Protein: 59
Carbs: 18
Fiber: 4.6
Fat: 19

Top Round w/ Bacon, Bourbon, + Potatoes

Serves: 6
Time: 1 hour, 30 minutes

This is an epic take on steak and potatoes. The top round becomes extremely tender in the pressure cooker, as do the beautiful Yukon Gold potatoes. The sauce is the real star - it's smoky, earthy, and just all-around rich.

Ingredients:

3 pounds beef top round
1 ½ pounds Yukon Gold potatoes
1 ½ cups beef broth
1 stemmed, cored, and chopped green bell pepper
4 chopped bacon slices
¼ cup bourbon
One, 6-inch rosemary sprig
2 teaspoons black pepper

Directions:

1. Roll the roast in the ground black pepper.
2. Turn your Instant Pot to "Sauté" and fry the bacon.
3. Move bacon to a plate.
4. Put the roast in the Instant Pot and brown all over.
5. Move the roast to the plate.
6. Add the bell pepper and soften for 3 minutes.
7. Pour beef broth into the pot, then the bourbon, and deglaze.
8. Toss in the rosemary sprig and then add the bacon and beef back into the pot.
9. Lock the lid.
10. Press "Manual," and then cook for 55 minutes on "high pressure."
11. When time is up, hit "Cancel" and quick-release.
12. Open the lid and add the potatoes.
13. Lock the lid.
14. Hit "Manual" again and cook for 15 minutes on "high pressure."
15. When time is up, press "Cancel" and let the pressure decrease naturally.

16. To serve, pick out the rosemary and take out the meat to rest for 5 minutes.
17. Slice, and serve with potatoes and lots of sauce.

Nutritional Info (⅙ recipe):

Total calories: 553
Protein: 73
Carbs: 21
Fiber: 1.6
Fat: 13

Chapter 9

Sides, Snacks, + Sauces

<u>Corn Pudding</u>

Serves: 4
Time: 45 minutes

This rich corn pudding highlights the natural sweetness of corn and would go beautifully with meat like pork or beef. Corn is at its peak May-September, so you should take advantage during those months.

<u>Ingredients:</u>

1 ½ cups water	¼ cup sour cream
2 chopped shallots	3 tablespoons cornmeal
1 cup fresh corn	1 tablespoon sugar
2 beaten eggs	Salt
¾ cup whole milk	Pepper

<u>Directions:</u>

1. Turn on your Instant Pot to "Sauté."
2. Add butter and melt.
3. Add shallots and hit "Cancel." The hot butter will cook the shallots.
4. While that cooks, mix corn, sour cream, cornmeal, milk, sugar, eggs, pepper, and salt in a bowl.
5. Add the melted butter and shallots and stir together.
6. Pour water into the Instant Pot and lower in the trivet.
7. Grease a 6-7 inch baking dish (round) and pour the corn pudding in.

8. Wrap in foil and place into the steamer rack.
9. Close the Instant Pot lid.
10. Press "Manual" and cook for 30 minutes at "low pressure."
11. When time is up, hit "Cancel" and quick-release the pressure.
12. Cool before serving.

Nutritional Info (¼ recipe):

Total calories -207
Protein - 6
Carbs - 19
Fiber - 1
Fat - 7

Beets w/ Goat Cheese

Serves: 4
Time: 30 minutes

For a simple, summer side dish or appetizer, these beets are fantastic. Beets are one of the healthiest foods out there, and when paired with creamy, tangy goat cheese, you'll want to keep eating one after another. You'll want to get fresh beets, not canned. Remember that beet juice stains everything, so wear gloves if you don't want to have to wash your hands for forever afterwards, and take care to not get any on your clothes.

Ingredients:

1 cup water
4 medium-sized, whole beets
½ cup crumbled goat cheese
½ lemon, juiced
Olive oil
Salt + pepper

Directions:

1. Pour water into the Instant Pot.
2. Lower in the steamer basket.
3. Wash and trim the beets.
4. Put them in the steamer basket and lock the Instant Pot lid.
5. Hit "Manual" and 20 minutes on "high pressure."
6. When time is up, quick-release the pressure.
7. Check the beets by poking them with a knife. If soft, they're done.
8. Run the beets under cold water and peel.
9. Slice.
10. To serve, plate the beets and sprinkle on the goat cheese, lemon juice, olive oil, salt, and pepper.

Nutritional Info (¼ recipe):

Total calories -112
Protein - 6
Carbs - 10

Fiber - 2
Fat - 4

Brown-Butter Fingerling Potatoes

Serves: 4
Time: 35 minutes

If you've never browned butter, you're really missing out. When you heat butter until it becomes an amber color, it becomes more fragrant and deeply-flavored, which is a perfect pairing to fingerling potatoes. A bit of rosemary at the end enhances the earthiness of the dish.

Ingredients:

1 ½ pounds small fingerling potatoes
½ cup chicken broth
2 tablespoons butter
Minced leaves of 1 small rosemary sprig
Salt + pepper

Directions:

1. Turn on the Instant Pot's "Sauté" function.
2. When hot, add the butter and melt.
3. When melted, add potatoes and stir.
4. Keep stirring for 10 minutes until the potato skins start to crisp up and the butter has become golden and nutty.
5. Pour in the broth and close the pot lid.
6. Hit "Manual" and 7 minutes on "high pressure."
7. When time is up, hit "Cancel" and wait for the pressure to decrease naturally for 10 minutes.
8. Quick-release any leftover pressure.
9. Open the lid.
10. Serve the potatoes with salt, pepper, and rosemary.

Nutritional Info (¼ recipe):

Total calories -175
Protein - 4
Carbs - 27
Fiber - 3
Fat - 4

Ricotta-Stuffed Zucchini

Serves: 6
Time: 7 minutes

Creamy ricotta makes a delicious filling for fresh summer zucchini. You mix the ricotta with breadcrumbs, nutmeg, thyme, and an egg yolk, and then stuff small logs of zucchini. The stuffed veggies cook for just 5 minutes in a bath of crushed tomatoes, oil, and onion, and you have the perfect appetizer ready to go.

Ingredients:

3 big zucchinis
1 ¾ cups crushed tomatoes
1 cup ricotta
1 yellow onion
½ cup breadcrumbs
2 tablespoons olive oil
1 tablespoon minced fresh oregano

1 large egg yolk
2 teaspoons minced garlic
2 teaspoons fresh thyme
¼ teaspoon grated nutmeg
Salt + pepper

Directions:

1. Mix breadcrumbs, ricotta, egg yolk, nutmeg, and thyme in a bowl.
2. Prepare the zucchini by cutting them into 2-inch long pieces. With a melon baller, hollow out the middles with about ¼-inch flesh on the sides and ½-inch on the bottom, so they don't fall apart.
3. Stuff 2 tablespoons of the ricotta mixture into the hollows.
4. Turn your Instant Pot to "Sauté," and cook onion until soft.
5. Add garlic and cook another 30 seconds.
6. Add oregano, tomatoes, salt, and pepper.
7. Put the zucchinis in the cooker, stuffed-side up.
8. Close and lock the lid.
9. Select "Manual," and then 5 minutes on "high pressure."
10. When time is up, hit "Cancel" and quick-release.
11. Serve with the sauce.

Nutritional Info (⅙ recipe):

Total calories: 209
Protein: 10
Carbs: 18
Fiber: 2
Fat: 11

Risotto w/ Peas + Brie Cheese

Serves: 6
Time: 10 minutes

A truly good side dish is one that could stand on its own, flavor-wise. This risotto using white Arborio rice, green peas, and creamy Brie cheese fits the profile. The rice is cooked in chicken broth, apple cider, and apple cider vinegar, and flavored with onion, sage, and nutmeg. The cheese and peas are added at the very end.

Ingredients:

4 cups chicken broth
1 ½ cups white Arborio rice
1 cup peas
4-ounces chopped Brie cheese, rind removed
¼ cup unsweetened apple cider

3 tablespoons butter
1 chopped yellow onion
1 tablespoon apple cider vinegar
1 tablespoon minced sage leaves
¼ teaspoon grated nutmeg

Directions:

1. Turn your Instant Pot to "Sauté" and melt the butter.
2. Toss in the chopped onion and soften for 4 minutes.
3. Add rice and stir until the rice is coated in butter.
4. Pour in apple cider and vinegar.
5. Stir until the rice has absorbed the liquid, which should take about 2 minutes.
6. Pour in the broth, and add sage and nutmeg.
7. Stir.
8. Close and secure the lid.
9. Select "Manual," and cook for 10 minutes on "high pressure."
10. When time is up, hit "Cancel" and quick-release.
11. Open the lid.
12. Stir in the peas and Brie cheese.
13. Close the lid to let the residual warmth melt the cheese and warm up the peas.
14. Stir right before serving.

Nutritional Info (⅙ recipe):

Total calories: 298
Protein: 9
Carbs: 44
Fiber: 3
Fat: 11

Asparagus + Rice w/ Brown Butter

Serves: 5-6
Time: 30 minutes

This satisfying side dish could really be a light meal in its own right, but it would also be perfect with a meat protein as the main attraction. You roast the asparagus in the oven, and cook the rice in the Instant Pot with brown butter, wine, broth, shallots, and garlic. Finish it all off with cream and cheese, and you've got a restaurant-quality result.

Ingredients:

4 cups chicken stock
2 cups Arborio rice
1 pound asparagus, cut into 1-inch pieces
5 tablespoons butter
4 minced garlic cloves
4 chopped shallots
½ cup dry white wine
½ cup grated Parmesan cheese
¼ cup cream
1 tablespoon olive oil
Salt + pepper

Directions:

1. Preheat your normal oven to 400-degrees.
2. Toss asparagus in olive oil, season, and layer on a baking sheet.
3. Roast for 10-15 minutes until tender and a bit crispy.
4. Turn your Instant Pot to "Sauté" and melt butter.
5. Stir occasionally until butter becomes brown and fragrant.
6. Toss in the shallots and cook for 2 minutes.
7. Add garlic and cook for another minute.
8. Pour in the wine and simmer until the wine has mostly evaporated.
9. Pour in the broth and rice.
10. Season before locking the Instant Pot lid.
11. Press "Manual" and then 6 minutes on "high pressure."
12. When time is up, hit "Cancel" and quick-release.
13. If there's still too much liquid, turn on "Sauté" and simmer.

14. Add cream and cheese.
15. Add the asparagus and serve!

Nutritional Info:

Total calories -441
Protein - 14
Carbs - 50
Fiber - 2
Fat - 11

Whole-Wheat Mac 'n Cheese

Serves: 12
Time: About 10 minutes

Mac 'n cheese is a classic Southern side dish, and whole-wheat pasta makes it even better. In the Instant Pot, this homemade recipe takes about as much time as anything from a box, *and* it uses familiar, affordable ingredients. Make this your go-to mac 'n cheese from now on.

Ingredients:

1 pound dry whole-wheat macaroni
4 cups water
10-ounces shredded sharp cheddar
8-ounces shredded Monterey Jack cheese
12-ounce can of evaporated milk
2-ounces grated Parmesan
1 cup breadcrumbs
3 tablespoons butter
1 tablespoon salt
1 teaspoon yellow mustard
¼ teaspoon black pepper

Directions:

1. Put the macaroni, mustard, salt, pepper, butter, and water into the Instant Pot and stir.
2. Lock the lid.
3. Press "Manual" and cook for half the time that the pasta box says. If the box recommends 10 minutes, cook in the Instant Pot for "4 minutes."
4. When the timer goes off, hit "Cancel" and quick-release.
5. If the pasta isn't done, just "Sauté" until it reaches your desired doneness.
6. With "Sauté" on, add the evaporated milk and stir.
7. Throw in the cheeses and stir until thoroughly blended.
8. Move the mac and cheese to a baking dish and sprinkle with breadcrumbs.
9. Broil in the oven for a few minutes.

10. Serve!

Nutritional Info (1/12 serving):

Total calories - 377
Protein - 19.5
Carbs - 32
Fiber - 3
Fat - 12.5

Classic Potato Salad

Serves: 8
Time: 10 minutes

Hard-boiling eggs and cooking potatoes for potato salad has never been faster. You cook both of them in the Instant Pot at once, and then just mix in some classic potato-salad ingredients like mayo, onion, parsley, and so on. It's a quick, tasty side dish that's perfect for summer.

Ingredients:

6 peeled and cubed russet potatoes
1 ½ cups water
4 eggs
1 cup mayonnaise
¼ cup chopped onion
2 tablespoons chopped parsley
1 tablespoon mustard
1 tablespoon dill pickle juice
Salt + pepper

Directions:

1. Pour water into the Instant Pot and lower in the steamer basket.
2. Put eggs and potatoes in the basket.
3. Lock the lid and hit "Manual," then "high pressure" for 4 minutes.
4. When time is up, hit "Cancel" and quick-release.
5. Put the eggs in ice water.
6. In a bowl, mix mayo, parsley, onion, mustard, and pickle juice.
7. Add the potatoes and mix.
8. Peel and cut eggs and mix into the potato salad.
9. Season.
10. Chill one hour before serving.

Nutritional Info (⅛ serving):

Total calories - 262
Protein - 5.3
Carbs - 30.8

Fiber - 2.9
Fat – 13

Broccoli Pesto

Makes: 2 ½ cups
Time: 20 minutes

Pesto is usually made with just basil and pine nuts, but for something a little different, there's this broccoli pesto with walnuts. If you don't care for basil, the broccoli provides a milder flavor, and goes great with pasta.

Ingredients:

1 pound broccoli florets
3 cups water
3 minced garlic cloves
1 cup fresh basil leaves
⅓ cup toasted walnuts
¼ cup olive oil
¼ cup grated Parmesan
2 tablespoons lemon juice
Salt + pepper

Directions:

1. Add broccoli and water to Instant Pot.
2. Press "Manual" and cook for 3 minutes on "high pressure."
3. While that cooks, pulse walnuts and garlic in a food processor.
4. When crumbly, stop.
5. When the pot timer goes off, hit "Cancel."
6. Quick-release the pressure in the Instant Pot.
7. Take out the broccoli and rinse in cold water.
8. Drain and pulse in the food processor with oil, basil, and lemon juice.
9. Pulse and add ¼ cup of cooking liquid, cheese, salt, and pepper.
10. Keep pulsing until smooth, adding cooking liquid if needed.
11. Serve with pasta.

Nutritional Info (½ cup serving):

Total calories - 248
Protein - 9
Carbs - 10
Fiber - 4
Fat - 3

<u>Cranberry Sauce</u>

Makes: 2 cups
Time: 35 minutes

Cranberries are in season during the fall, which is when you make cranberry sauce. It can be a messy process and take a long time, but with the Instant Pot, you can make the Thanksgiving staple in just 35 minutes or so.

<u>Ingredients:</u>

4 cups washed cranberries
1 cup sugar
1-inch peeled and sliced ginger
½ cup orange juice
Zest from ½ orange
Juice and zest from ½ lemon

<u>Directions:</u>

1. Put cranberries, sugar, orange juice, orange zest, ginger, lemon juice, and lemon zest into the Instant Pot.
2. Close the lid.
3. Hit "Manual" and then 15 minutes on "high pressure."
4. When time is up, press "Cancel" and wait 10 minutes for the pressure to come down.
5. If there's any leftover, release it.
6. Let the sauce cool.
7. Pick out the ginger if you want.
8. Store in the fridge for up to 3 weeks.

Nutritional Info (⅓ cup serving):

Total calories - 177
Protein - 0
Carbs - 43
Fiber - 3
Fat - 0

Italian-Style Meat Sauce

Serves: 6-8
Time: 1 hour, 15 minutes

Making your own spaghetti sauce from scratch is not only healthier than store-bought, it's much tastier. This Instant Pot sauce is packed with two kinds of sausage - spicy and sweet - and fresh herbs. Really good homemade sauce usually takes hours and hours of simmering, but in the pressure cooker, you can have it ready in about an hour and 15 minutes.

Ingredients:
3 crushed garlic cloves
1 peeled and diced carrot
1 diced celery stalk
1 diced onion
1 tablespoon olive oil
½ teaspoon salt
¼ teaspoon crushed red pepper flakes

1 ¼ pounds sweet Italian sausage
1 ¼ pounds hot Italian sausage
1 cup chicken broth
½ cup red wine
28-ounce can crushed tomatoes
2-3 sprigs fresh thyme
1 sprig fresh basil
1 sprig rosemary
1 teaspoon black pepper

Directions:

1. Let's focus on the first ingredient list, beginning by heating the oil in the Instant Pot on "Sauté."
2. Throw in the celery, carrot, onion, and garlic.
3. Add the salt and red pepper flakes immediately after, and stir for about 8 minutes, or until the onion has softened.
4. Pour in the wine and deglaze the pot.
5. Simmer for 1 minute.
6. Time for the second ingredient list. Add the raw sausage and brown

for 5 minutes.
7. Pour in the chicken broth and crushed tomatoes.
8. To make it easier to pick them out later, tie the herb sprigs together before adding to the pot.
9. Close and lock the Instant Pot lid.
10. Select "Manual," and then 20 minutes at "high pressure."
11. Sprinkle in the black pepper.
12. Serve!

Nutritional Info (1 cup serving):

Total calories - 302
Protein - 20
Carbs - 6
Fiber - 1
Fat - 21

Homemade BBQ Sauce

Makes: 2 ½ cups
Time: 20 minutes

You think "BBQ," you probably think slow and long. This BBQ sauce may taste like it's been simmering for hours, but it's actually just been cooked for about 10 minutes. Ingredients like liquid smoke, ginger, and cumin give it a smoky taste, while honey and vinegar add sweetness and brightness.

Ingredients:

1 chopped onion
¾ cup prunes
½ cup water
½ cup tomato puree
4 tablespoons vinegar
4 tablespoons honey
1 tablespoon sesame seed oil
1 teaspoon liquid smoke
1 teaspoon hot sauce
1 teaspoon salt
½ teaspoon ground ginger
⅛ teaspoon cumin

Directions:

1. Turn your pressure cooker to "Sauté."
2. Add the oil and onion.
3. Cook and stir occasionally until the edges of the onion brown.
4. In a mixing bowl, pour in water, tomato puree, vinegar, and honey.
5. Add in garlic, hot sauce, salt, liquid smoke, ginger, and cumin.
6. Mix everything well, so the honey dissolves.
7. Pour into the pressure cooker and add prunes.
8. Lock the pressure cooker lid.
9. Hit "Manual," and then 10 minutes on "high pressure."
10. When the timer goes off, hit "Cancel" and quick-release.
11. Blend the sauce well till smooth.

Nutritional Info (1 tablespoon serving):

Total calories - 20
Protein - 0
Carbs - 4.5
Fiber - .3
Fat - .4

Goat Cheese Mashed Potatoes

Serves: 8-10
Time: 45 minutes

Take mashed potatoes to the next level with herbed goat cheese. The result is just a little tangy, rich, and oh-so-creamy. Just throw whole Yukon Gold potatoes in the Instant Pot to cook in less than a half hour before adding the dairy products. It all finishes off in the broiler for a golden-brown top.

Ingredients:

3 pounds scrubbed Yukon Gold potatoes
8-ounces goat cheese w/ herbs
½ cup sour cream
½ cup milk
2 tablespoons butter
1 tablespoon salt
Pepper to taste

Directions:

1. Put the potatoes with 1 tablespoon of salt into the pressure cooker.
2. Pour in just enough water so they are halfway covered.
3. Close the lid.
4. Choose "Manual," and then 20 minutes on "high pressure."
5. When the timer beeps, hit "Cancel" and wait for the pressure to come down on its own.
6. When ready, take out the potatoes and drain.
7. Return to the pot, along with milk, sour cream, butter, and ¾ of the goat cheese.
8. Mash everything well to your desired consistency.
9. Scoop out the mashed potatoes into an 8-inch baking dish.
10. Swirl on the rest of the goat cheese on top.
11. Broil in the oven for 5 minutes.
12. Devour!

Nutritional Info (1/10 recipe):

Total calories - 254
Protein - 8.5
Carbs - 36
Fiber - 3.6
Fat - 8.5

Butternut Squash

Serves: 8
Time: 35 minutes

Butternut squash is one of my favorite vegetables. Not only are they healthy and packed with fiber, but they're also delicious. They're so naturally creamy, and can be seasoned to either be more savory or sweet.

Ingredients:

One butternut squash
1 cup of water
Salt
Pepper
Nutmeg

Directions:

1. Pour 1 cup of water into your Instant Pot and lower the steamer rack inside.
2. Wash the butternut squash.
3. Cut so it can fit in the pot.
4. When the squash is in the pot, close and lock the lid.
5. Push "Manual" and cook for 17 minutes on "high pressure."
6. When the timer beeps, hit "Cancel" and quick-release the pressure.
7. Open the lid so the squash can cool for 5 minutes.
8. If the squash is cut in half, take out the seeds from the bottom part and cut in half again.
9. If the top part is big, cut that in half, too.
10. Poke the squash to determine how cooked it is. If the squash still has a way to go, return the squash to the Pot and cook for another 17 minutes.
11. When time is up, hit "Cancel" and quick-release again.
12. Carefully take out the squash, scoop, mash, and season. Some salt, pepper, and nutmeg are a good start.

Nutritional Info (1 cup serving):

Total calories - 63
Protein - 1.4
Carbs - 16
Fiber - 2.8
Fat – 0

Brown-Sugar Carrots

Serves: 2
Time: About 20 minutes

If you or your kids don't like vegetables, these sweet carrots will change your tune. Coated in butter and brown sugar, the carrots are steamed for just 15 minutes. They're a great side dish to just about any meal I can think of.

Ingredients:

2 cups carrots
½ cup water
1 tablespoon brown sugar
½ tablespoon butter
Dash of salt

Directions:

1. Put the butter, brown sugar, salt, and water into the Instant Pot.
2. Hit the "sauté" button and stir until the butter melts.
3. Throw in the carrots and stir them around.
4. Close the lid.
5. Hit "Steam" and select 15 minutes.
6. When time is up, press "Cancel" and then quick-release.
7. Open up the lid and sauté until all the liquid is gone.
8. Take out the carrots and serve!

Nutritional Info (1 cup serving):

Total calories - 104
Protein - 1
Carbs - 19
Fiber - 3.4
Fat - 4

Quick Baked Potatoes

Serves: 4
Time: 30 minutes

Baked potatoes usually take forever. You have to time everything else around them, and sometimes, it's just not worth it. In the pressure cooker, free up the oven and have perfectly-baked potatoes in just 30 minutes.

Ingredients:

1 cup of water
Up to 5 pounds of potatoes (4 potatoes for 4 servings)
Seasonings

Directions:

1. Pour water into the Instant Pot and lower in the steamer rack.
2. Add the potatoes and secure the lid.
3. Click "Manual" and then the "-" button to 10 minutes.
4. When time is up, hit "Cancel" and wait 20 minutes for the pressure to come down on its own.
5. Open the lid and serve potatoes.

Nutritional Info (1 potato):

Total calories - 110
Protein - 4
Carbs - 26
Fiber - 2
Fat - 0

Buttery Orange Brussels Sprouts

Serves: 8
Time: 5 minutes

Brussels sprouts get a bad rap, and that's because people don't always know how to cook them. In the Instant Pot, they're wonderfully tender, and a buttery, zesty-sweet sauce made from orange juice, maple syrup, and butter counters any bitterness from the veggie.

Ingredients:

2 pounds Brussels sprouts
¼ cup orange juice
2 tablespoons maple syrup
1 tablespoon butter
1 teaspoon grated orange zest
½ teaspoon salt
¼ teaspoon black pepper

Directions:

1. Trim ¼ off of the bottom of every sprout and rinse in cold water.
2. Put them in the pressure cooker.
3. Cover with ¾ cup water.
4. Secure the lid to the Instant Pot.
5. Hit "Manual" and then 4 minutes.
6. While the sprouts cook, mix the sauce ingredients in a skillet over low heat, just to melt the butter and get the maple syrup integrated.
7. When the timer beeps, hit "Cancel" and quick-release.
8. Serve coated in sauce.

Nutritional Info (⅛ serving):

Total calories - 65
Protein - 3
Carbs - 12
Fiber - 3
Fat - 2

Red Beans

Serves: 8
Time: Overnight soak + 35 minutes

These beans are extremely flavorful and cooked with delicious Cajun ingredients like smoked sausage, onion, garlic, and celery. You can have the final product by itself as a side, or add cooked white rice for a complete protein.

Ingredients:

2 quarts water
1 pound rinsed red kidney beans
1 tablespoon salt

5 cups water
1 pound smoked sausage, cut into quarters lengthwise and then cut into ¼-inch pieces
4 sliced garlic cloves
2 bay leaves
1 big minced onion
1 seeded and minced green bell pepper
1 minced celery stalk
1 teaspoon olive oil
1 teaspoon dried thyme
1 teaspoon kosher salt
½ teaspoon salt
Black pepper

Directions:

1. The night before you plan on having the beans, go through them and throw out any bad ones.
2. Pour 2 quarts of water into a big bowl, add beans and salt, and soak overnight.
3. The next day, cook the aromatics. Pour 1 teaspoon oil into the pressure cooker and heat.
4. When shiny, add the celery, onion, pepper, thyme, garlic, sausage, and ½ teaspoon salt.

5. Stir while it's cooking, for 8 minutes, until the sausage and onions are starting to brown.
6. Drain and rinse off the beans.
7. Put them in the pressure cooker along with 1 teaspoon of salt and bay leaves.
8. Secure the lid and hit "Manual." Select 15 minutes.
9. When time is up, hit "Cancel" and wait 20 minutes.
10. Open the cooker and pick out the bay leaves.
11. Take out 2 cups of the beans and liquid and blend until smooth.
12. Pour them back into the cooker.
13. You can simmer for another 15 minutes if you want, but it's not necessary.
14. Serve!

Nutritional Info (⅛ serving):

Total calories - 235
Protein - 11
Carbs - 11
Fiber - 14
Fat - 17

Simple Spaghetti Squash

Serves: 4
Time: 10 minutes

Spaghetti squash, which is named because when you scrape out the cooked insides, it looks like pasta, is a fantastic alternative to regular pasta. It has a similar texture, and mildly-sweet taste. You can serve it however you would serve pasta, with a variety of sauces or just some olive oil, salt, and pepper!

Ingredients:

One 3-pound spaghetti squash
1 cup water

Directions:

1. Cut off the end of the squash with the stem and then cut in half.
2. Scoop out the seeds.
3. Pour water into your Instant Pot and lower in the steamer basket.
4. Put the cut squash in the basket and secure the lid.
5. Hit "Manual" and then cook for 8 minutes on "high pressure."
6. When the timer goes off, hit "Cancel" and then quick-release.
7. When you can handle the squash without burning yourself, scrap the insides out with a fork.
8. Serve!

Nutritional Info (1-cup serving):

Total calories - 31
Protein - .6
Carbs - 7
Fiber - 1.5
Fat - .6

Cheesy Potatoes

Serves: 4
Time: 15 minutes

Cheesy potatoes are one of life's great joys. They are a staple for holidays like Thanksgiving and are delicious with cuts of pork. In the Instant Pot, they're on the table in 15 minutes.

Ingredients:

6 peeled and ⅛-inch thick sliced potatoes
1 cup chicken broth
1 cup shredded cheese
1 cup panko bread crumbs
½ cup sour cream
½ cup chopped onion
2 tablespoons butter + 3 tablespoons melted butter
Pepper
Salt

Directions:

1. Hit the "sauté" button on your Instant Pot and put in 2 tablespoons butter.
2. When melted, add the onion and cook for about 5 minutes.
3. Pour in 1 cup of chicken broth, salt, and pepper.
4. Lower in the steamer basket with the sliced potatoes inside.
5. Lock the lid.
6. Hit "Manual," and then select 5 minutes on "high pressure."
7. While the potatoes cook, melt 3 tablespoons of butter and mix with the panko.
8. Grease a 9x13 baking dish.
9. When the potatoes are ready, hit "Cancel" and quick-release.
10. Remove the potatoes and layer them in the baking dish.
11. In the pressure cooker, mix cheese and sour cream into the cooking liquid.
12. Pour over potatoes and stir so they're thoroughly coated.
13. Pour over the panko/butter topping.
14. Broil in the oven for 5-7 minutes.

Nutritional Info (¼ serving):

Total calories - 358
Protein - 11
Carbs - 32
Fiber - 2
Fat - 22

Chapter 10

Seafood

Steamed Crab Legs w/ Garlic Butter

Serves: 4
Time: 15 minutes

If you're craving seafood, these crab legs are quick and delicious, especially with the addicting garlic-butter dipping sauce. You can use fresh or frozen legs in the Instant Pot, and there's only a minute cooking difference.

Ingredients:

2 pounds crab legs, fresh or frozen
1 cup water
4 tablespoons salted butter
1 halved lemon
1 big minced garlic clove
1 teaspoon olive oil

Directions:

1. Pour water into the Instant Pot and insert the steamer basket.
2. Put the crab legs inside and lock the lid.
3. Hit "Steam" and 3 minutes at "high pressure" for fresh, and 4 minutes for frozen.
4. Take a saucepan and heat olive oil on the stove.
5. Toss in the garlic and cook for 1 minute.
6. Add the butter and stir to melt.
7. Turn off the heat and squeeze in lots of lemon juice.

8. When the Instant Pot timer beeps, hit "Cancel" and quick-release.
9. Serve the crab and dipping sauce!

Nutritional Info (¼ serving):

Total calories - 346
Protein - 44
Carbs - 2
Fiber - 0
Fat - 7

Tuna Noodles

Serves: 2
Time: About 20 minutes

You're familiar with tuna noodle casserole. This version is a little different with the addition of marinated artichoke hearts and feta cheese, giving the classic comfort food a more sophisticated taste without the sophisticated price.

Ingredients:
8 ounces of uncooked dry, wide egg noodles
1 ¼ cups water
1 can drained tuna
1 can diced tomatoes
1 jar drained (save the liquid!) marinated, chopped artichoke hearts
½ cup chopped red onion
1 tablespoon oil
Feta cheese
Dried parsley
Dried basil
Salt
Pepper

Directions:

1. Turn on your Instant Pot and hit "sauté."
2. Heat a little olive oil until shiny.
3. Toss in the chopped red onion and cook, stirring, for 2 minutes.
4. Add water, noodles, tomatoes, and seasonings.
5. Hit "Soup" and then 10 minutes.
6. When time is up, hit "Cancel" and quick-release the pressure.
7. Add the tuna, artichokes, and the saved liquid.
8. Hit "Sauté" and stir for 4 minutes.
9. Serve with feta cheese and parsley.

Nutritional Info (½ serving):

Total calories - 547
Protein - 8
Carbs - 18

Fiber - 2
Fat - 3

White Fish w/ Beer and Potatoes

Serves: 6
Time: 40 minutes

Hearty, easy, and delicious, this recipe hits all the marks. You just throw everything into the Instant Pot, hit one button, and you're done!

Ingredients:

1 pound white fish (like cod or pollock)
4 peeled and diced potatoes
1 cup beer
1 sliced red pepper
1 tablespoon sugar
1 tablespoon oil
1 tablespoon oyster sauce
1 teaspoon salt

Directions:

1. Put everything in the Instant Pot.
2. Secure the lid.
3. Push "Bean/Chili."
4. Cook for 40 minutes.
5. When time is up, quick-release.
6. Serve and enjoy!

Nutritional Info (⅙ serving):

Total calories - 172
Protein - 16
Carbs - 22
Fiber - 2
Fat - 2

Spicy Lemon Salmon

Serves: 4
Time: About 5 minutes

Salmon is a superfood. It reduces your risk of heart disease and is just plain delicious. Nanami Togarashi is an Asian assorted chili pepper spice that you can find on Amazon or Asian markets. You can also just use ground spices of your own if you don't want to go out of your way, like ground ginger, red pepper, and so on.

Ingredients:
3-4, 1-inch thick salmon fillets
1 cup water
1 juiced lemon
1 sliced lemon
1-2 tablespoons Nanami Togarashi
Sea salt
Pepper

Directions:

1. Season the salmon generously with lemon juice, spices, pepper, and salt.
2. Lower the steamer rack into the Instant Pot and pour in 1 cup of water.
3. Place the fillets in the rack, without overlapping.
4. Secure the Instant Pot lid.
5. Hit "Manual" and then "-" until you get to 5 minutes.
6. Seal the lid.
7. When ready, quick-release the pressure.
8. Serve!

Nutritional Info (¼ serving):

Total calories - 118
Protein - 24
Carbs - 1
Fiber - 0
Fat - 2

One-Pot Shrimp Scampi

Serves: 4
Time: 5 minutes

Shrimp scampi can be a weekday dinner now. It's unbelievably fast when you cook it in the Instant Pot. You use frozen shrimp, and there's no cleaning or peeling required. The rice cooks right in with everything, making this a true one-pot, 5-minute meal.

Ingredients:

1 pound frozen wild-caught shrimp
1 cup jasmine rice
1 ½ cups water
4 minced garlic cloves
¼ cup chopped parsley
¼ cup butter
1 medium, juiced lemon
1 pinch saffron
Salt
Pepper
Red pepper flakes

Directions:

1. Mix everything in your pressure cooker, leaving the shells on the shrimp.
2. Close the lid and select "Manual," and 5 minutes on "high pressure."
3. When time is up, quick-release.
4. When you can touch the shrimp, peel off the shells.
5. Serve with parsley and grated cheese.

Nutritional Info (¼ serving):
Total calories - 225   Fiber - 0
Protein - 14   Fat – 12
Carbs - 10

Seafood Gumbo

Serves: 6-8
Time: 75 minutes

If you love seafood, gumbo is like the Holy Grail. It's full of shrimp, crab, and oysters, and flavored with smoky sausage, peppers, onion, and garlic. This recipe can serve a crowd. The whole process of preparing the ingredients and then cooking takes about 75 minutes, though the gumbo itself cooks in just a half hour.

Ingredients:

6 cups fish stock
1 pound crab meat
1 pound peeled and cleaned shrimp
24 shucked oysters
2 chopped smoked sausages
3 chopped celery stalks
2 chopped red bell peppers
1 chopped onion
½ cup flour
½ cup chopped green onions
½ cup veggie oil
¼ cup chopped parsley
2 tablespoons dried thyme
2 tablespoons minced garlic cloves
Salt and pepper to taste

Directions:

1. Turn on your Instant Pot to "sauté" and pour in 2 tablespoons of vegetable oil.
2. Add red pepper, celery, garlic, and onions.
3. When the veggies are browned, pour in the fish stock and add sausages, pepper, and thyme.
4. Close the Instant Pot lid and hit "Manual" and then 10 minutes.
5. When time is up, hit "Cancel." Quick-release.
6. In another skillet, heat up the rest of the oil and mix in the flour to make a roux.
7. Stir constantly until the flour becomes golden.

8. Take the skillet off the heat and mix in a bowl with some fish stock.
9. Pour into the Instant Pot and stir until the gumbo thickens.
10. Throw in the shrimp, oysters, and crab.
11. Lock the lid again and cook for just 1 minute on high pressure.
12. Quick-release.
13. Serve the gumbo with greens onions, parsley, and rice.

Nutritional Info (⅙ serving):

Total calories - 135
Protein - 13
Carbs - 5
Fiber - 0
Fat - 7

Scallop Chowder

Serves: 4-6
Time: 10 minutes

This quick-cooking chowder uses sweet bay scallops, heavy cream, and white wine for a truly authentic, New England taste. The bacon adds smokiness, while herbs like thyme, chives, and parsley keep things fresh.

Ingredients:

2 pounds cut Yukon Gold
1 ½ pounds bay scallops
3 thin bacon slices
2 chopped celery stalks
1 chopped yellow onion
2 cups chicken broth
1 cup heavy cream
1 cup clam juice
½ cup dry white wine
¼ cup chopped parsley
2 bay leaves
2 tablespoons butter
2 tablespoons minced chives
1 tablespoon fresh thyme leaves

Directions:

1. Fry the bacon in your Instant Pot on the "Sauté" setting.
2. Move to a plate.
3. Add butter to the pot and melt.
4. Toss in celery and onion. Cook until soft.
5. Pour in clam juice, broth, and wine.
6. Deglaze.
7. Add potatoes, thyme, and bay leaves.
8. Secure and lock the lid.
9. Hit "Manual," and select "high pressure" for 7 minutes.
10. When time is up, hit "Cancel" and quick-release.
11. Open the lid.
12. Stir and turn to the "Sauté" setting.

13. Crumble in the bacon and add scallops, cream, chives, and parsley.
14. Cook for 2 minutes while stirring the whole time.
15. Pick out bay leaves.
16. Serve!

Nutritional Info (¼ recipe):

Total calories: 396
Protein: 26.7
Carbs: 46.1
Fiber: 3.9
Fat: 13.1

Shrimp + Corn Stew

Serves: 4
Time: 10 minutes

Even during the summer, this stew is light and fresh enough to enjoy. It has shrimp, which you can buy fresh or frozen, corn, bacon, onion, and a bell pepper. It's lighter than stews with potatoes, and only takes about five minutes in the Instant Pot.

Ingredients:

1 pound peeled and cleaned shrimp, cut in half
2 cups chicken broth
1 cup corn kernels
2 chopped bacon slices
1 chopped yellow onion
1 stemmed, cored, and chopped yellow bell pepper
½ cup heavy cream
2 tablespoons butter
1 tablespoon minced oregano leaves
2 teaspoons lemon zest
½ teaspoon celery seeds

Directions:

1.   Turn your Instant Pot to "Sauté" and melt the butter.
2.   Cook the bacon for about 3 minutes, until crispy.
3.   Add bell pepper and onion. Cook until softened.
4.   Toss in the lemon zest, oregano, and celery seeds, and cook for about 30 seconds.
5.   Pour in the broth.
6.   Stir before locking the lid.
7.   Select "Manual," and then 5 minutes on "high pressure."
8.   When time is up, hit "Cancel" and quick-release.
9.   Open the cooker.
10. Turn the pot back to "Sauté."
11. Stir in the corn, cream, and shrimp.
12. Keep stirring as the shrimp cooks, which should take about 3 minutes, or until the shrimp becomes firm and pink.

13. Serve!

Nutritional Info (¼ recipe):

Total calories: 258
Protein: 19
Carbs: 12
Fiber: 1
Fat: 15

Clam Rolls

Serves: 4
Time: 5 minutes

Missing the beach? These clam rolls will take you right there. Cooking the clams only takes 4 minutes in the Instant Pot, and then you dress them in a tangy, creamy mixture of mayo, Greek yogurt, lemon juice, celery, and other seasonings.

Ingredients:

4 hot dog buns
8 romaine lettuce leaves
24 scrubbed littleneck clams
3 sliced celery stalks
1 stemmed, cored, and chopped red bell pepper
4 tablespoons melted and cooled butter
¼ cup plain Greek yogurt
¼ cup mayonnaise
2 tablespoons lemon juice
½ teaspoon black pepper
½ teaspoon dried dill

Directions:

1. Pour 1 ½ cups water into the Instant Pot and add the clams.
2. Close and lock the lid.
3. Select "Manual," and then "high pressure" for 4 minutes.
4. When time is up, hit "Cancel" and quick-release.
5. Pour the Instant Pot contents into a colander in a sink.
6. Cool.
7. In a bowl, mix the bell pepper, yogurt, mayo, celery, lemon juice, pepper, dill, and a few dashes of hot sauce.
8. Pull the meat from their shells, chop, and mix into the dressing.
9. Brush the inside of the hot dog buns with butter.
10. Heat a skillet and toast the buns.
11. Fill buns with lettuce and clam salad.

Nutritional Info (¼ recipe):

Total calories: 408
Protein: 17
Carbs: 29
Fiber: 1
Fat: 26

Lobster Casserole

Serves: 4
Time: 10 minutes

Lobster and pasta cook together in the Instant Pot for just 8 minutes before you add in a rich sauce made from half-and-half, wine, Worcestershire, and tarragon. You finish it off with Gruyere cheese, and end up with a delicious casserole that tastes like the weekend, but cooks quickly like a weekday meal.

Ingredients:

6 cups water
Three, 6-ounce lobster tails
8-ounces dried ziti
1 cup half-and-half
¾ cup Gruyere cheese
½ cup dry white wine
1 tablespoon chopped tarragon leaves
1 tablespoon Worcestershire sauce
1 tablespoon flour
½ teaspoon black pepper

Directions:

1. Pour 6 cups of water into the Instant Pot.
2. Add lobster tails and pasta.
3. Lock the lid.
4. Select "Manual," and then cook for 8 minutes on "high pressure."
5. When time is up, hit "Cancel" and quick-release.
6. Drain the pasta and lobster in a colander in the sink.
7. Cool.
8. Take out the meat from their shells, chop, and put back into the pasta.
9. Turn the Instant Pot to "Sauté."
10. Pour in wine, half-and-half, Worcestershire, tarragon, flour, and pepper.
11. Let the liquid simmer while stirring, so the flour dissolves.
12. Add pasta and lobster back into pot, stirring for 30 seconds.

13. Sprinkle on the cheese and stir until melted.
14. Hit "Cancel" and cover halfway with the lid, so the casserole thickens.
15. Serve hot!

Nutritional Info (¼ recipe):

Total calories: 441
Protein: 28
Carbs: 44
Fiber: 0
Fat: 15

Chapter 11

Vegan

Vegan Strawberries + Cream Oats

Serves: 2
Time: 13 minutes

It's easy to make this classic flavor combo vegan. Simply replace regular milk with a non-dairy version. I like coconut milk, because it's exceptionally creamy and good for you! You can also sub out other fruit for the strawberries for what's in season if you want.

Ingredients:

6 large strawberries
2 cups of water
1 cup steel-cut oats
1 cup full-fat coconut milk
½ vanilla bean

Directions:

1. Scrape the vanilla bean so you get the seeds out.
2. Add everything (except the strawberries) to your Instant Pot, including the vanilla bean pod.
3. Select "Manual" on your pot and decrease the time to 3 minutes at "high pressure."
4. When time is up, unplug the cooker and wait 10 minutes.
5. Cut up the strawberries and serve.
6. To sweeten, use a vegan-friendly option like maple syrup or agave.

Nutritional Info:

Total calories - 264
Protein - 5
Carbs - 31
Fiber - 10
Fat – 13

Buckwheat Porridge w/ Rice Milk

Serves: 3-4
Time: 26 minutes

Buckwheat is a very healthy alternative to regular oats; it's technically a seed. That makes this recipe gluten-free as well as vegan. There's also no sugar, except the natural sugar in bananas, raisins, and vanilla.

Ingredients:

3 cups rice milk
1 cup raw buckwheat groats
¼ cup raisins
1 sliced banana
1 teaspoon ground cinnamon
½ teaspoon vanilla

Directions:

1. Rinse the buckwheat and put in the Instant Pot.
2. Pour in rice milk, and add raisins, bananas, vanilla, and cinnamon.
3. Lock the lid.
4. Select "Manual," and then "high pressure" for 6 minutes.
5. When time is up, hit "Cancel" and wait for the pressure to come down naturally.
6. Open the lid and stir.
7. Serve with a little more rice milk and any desired toppings.

Nutritional Info (¼ recipe):

Total calories - 297
Protein - 6
Carbs - 66
Fiber - 4
Fat - 3

Vegan Yogurt

Makes: 2 pints
Time: 12+ hours

Vegans can't have dairy, and it can be difficult when you're missing out on creamy delicious foods like yogurt. Well, you can make vegan yogurt in your Instant Pot with soy milk and a vegan yogurt starter from a company like Cultures for Health.

Ingredients:

1 quart room-temperature organic plain soy milk
1 packet Cultures for Health vegan yogurt starter

Directions:

1. Pour the soy milk into a pitcher and stir in yogurt starter.
2. Pour into two clean pint jars.
3. Put jars into the Instant Pot.
4. Lock the lid.
5. Hit "Yogurt" and set for 12 hours.
6. When time is up, hit "Cancel" and let the pressure come down on its own for 20 minutes. Carefully quick-release the rest of the pressure.
7. Chill in the fridge overnight before serving.

Nutritional Info (½ cup recipe):

Total calories - 50
Protein - 4
Carbs - 4
Fiber - .5
Fat - 2

No-Dairy Mashed Potatoes

Serves: 8
Time: About 20 minutes

Mashed potatoes are usually made with lots of cream and butter, so to make it vegan-friendly, this recipe uses dairy-free Earth Balance and a pureed pine nut mixture. Soy milk is added at the end to really get that creamy texture everyone loves from mashed potatoes.

Ingredients:

4 pounds of peeled and rinsed red + yellow potatoes
1 ½ cups water + ½ cup water
2 tablespoons olive oil Earth Balance
⅛ cup pine nuts
1 teaspoon salt
Soy milk

Directions:

1. Pour 1 ½ cups of water into your Instant Pot, lower in the trivet, and add the potatoes.
2. Press "Steam" and then 15 minutes on "high pressure."
3. As the potatoes cook, puree ½ cup water and pine nuts.
4. When the pot timer goes off, quick-release the cooker.
5. Take out the potatoes and roughly chop in a bowl.
6. Add the pine nut mixture, Earth balance, ¼ cup soy milk, and salt to the bowl.
7. Mash till smooth, adding soy milk as needed.

Nutritional Info (⅛ recipe):

Total calories - 213
Protein - 5
Carbs - 41

Fiber - 3
Fat – 5

Minestrone Soup

Serves: 4-6
Time: 18 minutes

Every cook needs to have mastered at least one soup recipe. This minestrone is a great one to learn by heart - it's easy, healthy, and delicious. In the Instant Pot, it takes less than 20 minutes.

Ingredients:

28-ounce can of tomatoes
3 minced garlic cloves
4 cups veggie broth
2 cups cooked white beans
2 diced celery stalks
½ cup fresh spinach, torn
1 bay leaf
1 diced onion
1 diced carrot
1 cup elbow pasta
2 tablespoons olive oil
1 teaspoon dried basil
1 teaspoon dried oregano
Salt + pepper

Directions:

1. Turn your Instant Pot to "Sauté."
2. Add in the olive oil, carrot, celery, garlic, and onion.
3. When softened, add in basil, oregano, pepper, and salt.
4. Pulse the can of tomatoes (along with its liquid) in a processor to break them down.
5. Pour into the pot, along with broth, spinach, pasta, and the bay leaf.
6. Secure the Instant Pot lid and press "Manual," and then 6 minutes on "high pressure."
7. When the timer beeps, hit "Cancel" and wait 2 minutes.
8. Quick-release.
9. Add in the beans and stir.
10. Serve!

Nutritional Info:

Total calories - 82
Protein - 4.3
Carbs - 11
Fiber - 1
Fat - 2.5

Three-Bean Chili

Serves: 6-8
Time: About 26-30 minutes

Who says vegan food has to leave you hungry? This hearty chili is full of beans and spices like cumin, garlic, and smoked paprika. You won't miss meat at all, and even though it only takes just over a half-hour, the flavors will taste like they've been simmering for ages.

Ingredients:

3 ½ cups vegetable broth
2 cups chopped onion
1 ½ cups of cooked black beans
1 ½ cups cooked red beans
1 ½ cups cooked pinto beans
¾ cup chopped carrots
¼ cup chopped celery
14.5-ounces of diced tomatoes
14.5-ounces of tomato sauce
1 chopped red bell pepper
2 tablespoons mild chili powder
1 tablespoon minced garlic
1 ½ teaspoons dried oregano
1 ½ teaspoons cumin
1 teaspoon cumin seeds
1 teaspoon smoked paprika
½ teaspoon coriander

Directions:

1. Drain and rinse the beans.
2. In your Instant Pot, select "sauté" and cook the cumin seeds, onion, and minced garlic for 5 minutes. Pour in vegetable broth to avoid burning the spices.
3. Once fragrant, add in everything except the tomatoes and tomato sauce.
4. Stir before securing the lid.
5. Select "Manual" and choose 6 minutes on "high pressure."
6. When time is up, unplug the cooker (or press "cancel") and wait 10

minutes for the pressure to decrease naturally.

7. Open the lid and stir in the tomatoes and tomato sauce.
8. Let the chili rest and thicken, leaving the lid off.
9. When it reaches your desired texture, serve with toppings like green onions, parsley, vegan cheese, and so on.

Nutritional Info (⅙ recipe):

Total calories - 456
Protein - 27.6
Carbs - 80
Fiber - 24
Fat - 4

Vegan Feijoada

Serves: 6
Time: 40 minutes (+ overnight soak time)

Feijoada is usually made with beef, pork, and beans, but this vegan version substitutes the meat with soy curls, vegan sausage, and lots of veggies. It's a great side dish or protein-heavy snack for days when you need an extra boost.

Ingredients:

2 ½ cups veggie broth
2 cups dried black beans (soaked overnight)
1 cup soy curls (softened in hot water for 15 minutes and drained)
2 peeled and cut carrots
2 sliced onions
4 minced garlic cloves
2 bay leaves
1 chopped red bell pepper
1 spicy chopped vegan sausage
⅓ cup dry red wine
1 tablespoon cumin
½ tablespoon smoked paprika
½ tablespoon dried thyme
½ tablespoon liquid smoke
½ teaspoon black pepper

Directions:

1. Turn on your Instant Pot to "sauté" and pour in a little water.
2. Add onions, bell pepper, carrots, and garlic and stir for 5 minutes.
3. Add spices and cook for a few minutes.
4. Pour in the red wine, wait 2 minutes, and then add the sausage, broth, beans, soy curls, and bay leaves.
5. Stir.
6. Lock the pressure cooker.
7. Hit "Bean/Chile" and adjust time to 30 minutes.
8. When the timer goes off, hit "Cancel" and wait for the pressure to come down.
9. Carefully open the lid and make sure the beans are soft.

10. Serve with herbs like parsley or cilantro!

Nutritional Info (⅙ recipe):

Total calories - 328
Protein - 20
Carbs - 54
Fiber - 13
Fat - 4

Spicy-Sweet Braised Cabbage

Serves: 4
Time: About 10 minutes

Spicy and sweet are two great flavor combinations, and when added to tender cabbage leaves perfectly steamed in an Instant Pot, you have a delicious vegan side dish. Browning the cabbage wedges before pressure-cooking them is an important step, because it gives the finished product a richer "roasted" flavor usually missing from steamed veggies.

Ingredients:

1 ¼ cups of water + 2 teaspoons of water
3 pounds of cabbage, divided into 8 wedges
¾ cup grated carrots
¼ cup apple cider vinegar
1 tablespoon sesame oil
2 teaspoons cornstarch
1 teaspoon raw demerara sugar (Bob's Red Mill is a good brand)
½ teaspoon red pepper flakes
½ teaspoon cayenne powder

Directions:

1. Turn on the Instant Pot to the "sauté" function.
2. Pour in sesame oil and lay down the cabbage wedges to brown for 3 minutes on one side.
3. Remove the wedges.
4. Pour in 1 ¼ cups of water, sugar, cayenne, pepper flakes, and vinegar.
5. Return the cabbage wedges to the pot along with the grated carrot.
6. Secure the lid and select the "Manual" setting. Choose "high pressure" and cook for 5 minutes.
7. Quick-release the pressure.
8. Remove the cabbage wedges.
9. Turn the cooker back on to "sauté" and bring the cooking liquid to a bowl.
10. In a bowl, mix 2 teaspoons of *cold* water with the cornstarch.
11. Pour into the Instant Pot.
12. Keep boiling, allowing the liquid to thicken.

13. Pour over the cabbage wedges before serving.

Nutritional Info (¼ recipe):

Total calories - 127
Protein - 4
Carbs - 22
Fiber - 6
Fat -   4

Chipotle-Pumpkin Soup

Serves: 6
Time: 18 minutes

Looking for something hot and a little spicy? This vegan soup is perfect for fall and winter, and only takes about 20 minutes to throw together. Jam-packed with ingredients like red potatoes, pumpkin puree, chipotle, and seasonings like nutmeg and cinnamon, this recipe just tastes like autumn.

Ingredients:

2 cups veggie broth
2 cups water
2 cups diced red potatoes
2 cups diced green apples
15-ounce can of pumpkin puree
 1 diced onion
3 diced garlic cloves
1 seeded chipotle in adobe sauce
¼ cup uncooked red lentils run through a food processor
¼ cup walnuts run through a food processor
1 teaspoon salt
1 teaspoon black pepper
1 teaspoon cinnamon
¼ teaspoon nutmeg

Directions:

1. Turn on the Instant Pot's "sauté" setting and cook the garlic and onion for about 3-4 minutes.
2. When brown and fragrant, toss in all the spices, including the chipotle pepper, and stir.
3. Pour in the water and veggie broth, along with the potatoes, apples, pumpkin puree, and ground lentils and walnuts.
4. Choose the "Manual" setting and select a 4-minute cook time on "high pressure."
5. When the beep sounds, hit "Cancel" or unplug the cooker.
6. Wait 10 minutes for the pressure to come down by itself,
7. Before opening, release any leftover pressure.
8. Open up the lid and blend the soup, either with an immersion hand

blender, or by carefully pouring it into a blender.
9.   When smooth, serve right away!

Nutritional Info:

Total calories - 147
Protein - 5
Carbs - 26.5
Fiber - 4.2
Fat - 3.7

Sweet Potato + Kidney Bean Stew

Serves: 6
Time: About 25 minutes

Seasoned with red curry paste, garlic, and green chilis, this sweet potato + kidney bean-based stew will satisfy your hunger and your taste buds. If it sounds too spicy for you, you can reduce ingredients like the chili powder.

Ingredients:

1.5 pounds of diced sweet potatoes
4 cups veggie broth
2, 15-ounce cans of cooked kidney beans (drained and rinsed)
28-ounces of diced tomatoes (with liquid)
1, 15-ounce can of full-fat coconut milk

1 cup of dried brown lentils
½ cup chopped cilantro
2 minced garlic cloves
1 big diced onion
1 can green chilis
2 tablespoons red curry paste
2 tablespoons chili powder
1 tablespoon lime juice
1 teaspoon sea salt

Directions:

1. Select the "Sauté" setting on the Instant Pot and add garlic and onion.
2. When the aromatics are soft, add the sweet potatoes and stir for a few minutes.
3. Press "Cancel" and add the rest of the ingredients.
4. Secure the lid.
5. Choose "Manual" and a cook time of 10 minutes on "high pressure."
6. When the timer beeps, hit "Cancel" again and wait 10 minutes.
7. Quick-release any remaining pressure.
8. Stir and serve right away!

Nutritional Info:

Total calories - 111
Protein - 5
Carbs - 23

Fiber - 5
Fat - 8

Vegan Taco Mix

Serves: 8
Time: Overnight + about 45 minutes

This versatile taco mix is meat-free, tasty, and healthy. You can wrap it in a corn tortilla, have a lettuce wrap, or serve it over greens as a salad. You can even eat it straight out of a bowl if you want. The dried beans need to be soaked overnight, so just plan accordingly.

Ingredients:

1 pound soaked dried pinto beans
3 cups water
2 chopped garlic cloves
1 chopped medium-sized onion
2 whole dried red chilis

2 tablespoons tomato paste
1 minced green pepper
2 teaspoons oregano
2-3 teaspoons chili powder
½ teaspoon ground cumin
Salt

Directions:

1. The beans should be soaked overnight. The night before you plan on making this recipe, rinse the beans and cover them with water. Drape a cloth towel over the bowl and store on the counter.
2. The next day, drain the beans
3. Pour 3 cups of water into your Instant Pot and add the beans, along with the garlic, onion, oregano, chilies, and cumin.
4. Close the lid.
5. Select "Manual" and choose 5 minutes at "high pressure."
6. When ready, unplug the cooker and wait 10 minutes for the pressure to decrease naturally.
7. Open the cooker and take out the dried chilies.
8. Add the remaining ingredients and cook without the lid for another 20-30 minutes in order for the flavors to deepen.
9. Serve in a corn tortilla or on top of fresh lettuce.

Nutritional Info:
Total calories - 215
Protein - 12.9
Carbs - 39.5

Fiber - 10
Fat -   8

Spaghetti Squash Lasagna w/ Cashew Cheese Sauce

Serves: 6
Time: 1 hour, 30 minutes

Regular lasagna gets a major vegan makeover. Instead of noodles, you use spaghetti squash, which is almost identical to real spaghetti in terms of texture. The filling is made from tofu, garlic, and basil instead of the usual ricotta mix, while the cheese sauce is actually cashews and nut milk that have been blended together.

Ingredients:

3 pounds spaghetti squash
8-ounces sliced mushrooms
1 ½ cups spaghetti sauce
1 minced garlic clove
Salt and pepper to taste

1, 14-ounce package of extra-firm tofu (not silken)
2 peeled garlic cloves
2 tablespoons nutritional yeast
1 cup packed fresh basil

1 cup plain nut milk
¼ cup raw cashews
¼ cup nutritional yeast
2 tablespoons cornstarch
1 tablespoon lemon juice
½ teaspoon dry mustard

Directions:

1. Begin by pressure-cooking the squash. Cut it in half lengthwise and remove the seeds.
2. Pour 1 cup of water into your Instant Pot and lower in the steamer basket.
3. Put the squash in the basket.
4. Close the cooker.
5. Select "Manual," and then "high pressure" for 8 minutes.

6. Unplug the cooker and quick-release when time is up, and cool before removing the squash.
7. Scrape the spaghetti strands using a fork and store in a colander that's resting over a bowl.
8. Heat a stovetop saucepan and toss in the chopped garlic, mushrooms, and 1 tablespoon of water.
9. Stir and cover. Stir every minute or so for 3 minutes.
10. Take off the lid and cook until the liquid evaporates.
11. Season and set aside for now.
12. Put the 2 peeled garlic cloves in a food processor and chop.
13. Add the rest of the ingredients in the second ingredient list and process till creamy and smooth.
14. Using a blender, pour everything in the third ingredient list and smooth.
15. Time to assemble. Pour in ¼ cup of the spaghetti sauce along with ¼ cup of veggie stock in the pressure cooker. Put ½ of the spaghetti squash right on top.
16. Spoon the tofu filling over the squash and spread, so it's even.
17. Add mushrooms and then half of the cashew "cheese" sauce on top.
18. Add the rest of the squash and then the rest of the spaghetti sauce.
19. Close the Instant Pot lid.
20. Select "Manual" and cook for just 5 minutes on "low pressure." You're really just heating everything up.
21. When the timer beeps, let the pressure come down naturally for 10 minutes.
22. Open the cooker and pour the rest of the cashew "cheese" on top.
23. Let the lasagna rest for a few minutes before serving.

Nutritional Info:

Total calories - 254
Protein - 18.3
Carbs - 30.5
Fiber - 3.3
Fat - 8.4

Black-Eyed Peas + Kale Bowl

Serves: 6
Time: About 50 minutes

This super-bowl is insanely healthy and also delicious, with flavors like ginger, garlic, and soy-free coconut aminos, which is like a sweeter soy sauce. The Instant Pot cooks dried black-eyed beans very quickly, so you don't have to resort to canned beans for this dish.

Ingredients:

5 cups water + 2 tablespoons water
1 ½ cups of rinsed, dried black-eyed peas
1 tablespoon chopped garlic
1 tablespoon chopped ginger root + 2 teaspoons chopped ginger root
1 tablespoon coconut aminos
2 minced garlic cloves
½ teaspoon salt
¼ teaspoon red pepper flakes

2 cups brown rice
2 ½ cups water

1 big bunch of kale, with stems removed and leaves chopped up
1 minced garlic clove
1 chopped, small onion
½ chopped red bell pepper
¼ cup water
1 tablespoon coconut aminos

Directions:

1. Pour 5 cups of water into the Instant Pot.
2. Add the peas, 1 tablespoon of garlic, 1 tablespoon of ginger, and ½ teaspoon of salt.
3. Secure the lid and select "Manual," and then cook for 10 minutes at "high pressure."
4. When ready, unplug the cooker and wait 10 minutes before quick-releasing any remaining pressure.
5. Drain the peas, leaving 1 cup of the cooking liquid.

6. Take out a saucepan and pour the 2 tablespoons of water into it.
7. Heat over the stove.
8. Add 2 teaspoons of ginger root and the 2 cloves of garlic.
9. After two minutes of cooking, add ⅓ cup of the pea cooking liquid, the beans, 1 tablespoon coconut aminos, and red pepper flakes.
10. Now is a good time to make the brown rice. To make brown rice in the Instant Pot, pour in 2 ½ cups of water with 2 cups of brown rice.
11. Close the lid and choose "Manual," and then 22 minutes on "high pressure."
12. Let this simmer for 20-30 minutes, without a liquid. If the peas start to dry out, add more of their cooking liquid.
13. The rice should be done now. The pot will automatically go to "keep warm." Keep this position for 10 minutes before hitting "cancel" and quick-releasing any leftover steam. You can keep the rice in the cooker for now.
14. Take out another skillet and add the onion.
15. Cook until it starts to brown, and then add garlic and the red bell pepper.
16. Add the kale and ¼ cup of water and cover.
17. After 3-6 minutes, the kale should still be very green, but tender.
18. Take the skillet off the hot burner and add 1 tablespoon coconut aminos.
19. Serve the peas with the kale and rice. Sriracha is a good condiment.

Nutritional Info (⅙ recipe):

Total calories - 186
Protein - 12.5
Carbs - 34.4
Fiber - 6.2
Fat -   1

Sweet Potato Peanut Butter Soup

Serves: 4
Time: 10-15 minutes

Peanut butter in soup? Absolutely. The nutty butter is a perfect complement to the also-nutty, but sweeter sweet potatoes, and other flavors from the onion, garlic, lime, and chilis ensure you won't feel like you're eating a bowl of liquid peanuts.

Ingredients:

3 big sweet potatoes, cubed
3 chopped garlic cloves
1 chopped onion
15-ounce can of diced tomatoes (liquid saved)
14-ounce can of full-fat coconut milk

4-ounce can of green chilis
2 cups veggie broth
½ cup peanut butter
1 tablespoon lime juice
½ teaspoon allspice
¼ teaspoon ground cilantro

Directions:

1. Turn on the Instant Pot and hit "Sauté."
2. Pour in a little oil and cook the garlic and onion, stirring, until soft.
3. Hit "Cancel."
4. Add the rest of the ingredients and stir.
5. Lock the lid.
6. Press "Manual" and adjust time to 4 minutes on "high pressure."
7. When the timer beeps, hit "Cancel" again and wait for the pressure to decrease naturally.
8. Stir.
9. Puree until smooth and serve!

Nutritional Info (¼ recipe):

Total calories - 286
Protein - 8
Carbs - 29

Fiber - 6
Fat - 16

Vegan Chocolate Cheesecake

Serves: 8
Time: 6 hours

Cheesecake on a vegan diet? It sounds impossible, after all, the word "cheese" is in the name. However, it is possible to make a delicious, creamy cheesecake without any dairy by using ingredients like coconut oil, nut milk, and chocolate chips from a brand like Enjoy Life. Like all cheesecakes, there's a somewhat lengthy cooling and chilling process, so bear that in mind. *Note: Also remember that cashews should be soaked for at least 2 hours, though overnight is ideal.*

Ingredients:

1 ½ cups almond flour
¼ cup vegan sweetener
¼ cup melted coconut oil

1 ¾ cups water (for the Instant Pot)
1 ½ cups soaked and drained cashews
1 cup chocolate nut milk
⅔ cups sugar
¼ cup non-dairy chocolate chips
2 tablespoons coconut flour
2 teaspoons vanilla
½ teaspoon salt

Directions:

1. Mix the ingredients in the first list (the crust) and press into a silicone, 7-inch cheesecake pan, covering the bottom and a little way up the sides.
2. Store in the fridge while you're making the filling.
3. Mix all the ingredients (except the chips) in a blender for about 2 minutes or until smooth.
4. Add in the chips and mix again just to distribute them.
5. Pour the batter into the pan.
6. Pour 1 ¾ cups of water into the Instant Pot and lower in the trivet.
7. Place the cheesecake pan into the cooker and close the lead.
8. Select "Manual" and choose "high pressure" for 55 minutes.
9. When the timer beeps, unplug the cooker and wait 10 minutes.

10. Quick-release any leftover pressure.
11. Open the lid and carefully remove the pan.
12. Cool for 1 hour
13. Store in the fridge, covered, for at least 4 hours to chill.

Nutritional Info:

Total calories - 396
Protein - 8
Carbs - 36
Fiber - 1
Fat - 26

Chapter 12

Desserts

Chocolate-Chip Zucchini Bread w/ Walnuts

Serves: 24
Time: 35 minutes

This chocolate-chip bread is made with lots of grated zucchini, applesauce, and chopped walnuts, so it is rich, but not without healthy elements, too. You'll need a bundt pan; 8-inches fits perfectly into the Instant Pot.

Ingredients:

3 eggs
2 ½ cups flour
A little less than 2 cups of sugar
2 cups grated zucchini
1 cup applesauce
½ cup baking cocoa
½ cup chocolate chips
½ cup chopped walnuts
1 tablespoon pure vanilla extract
1 teaspoon baking soda
1 teaspoon salt
1 teaspoon cinnamon
¼ teaspoon baking powder

Directions:

1. In a bowl, beat the applesauce, vanilla, sugar, and eggs together.

2. Mix in the zucchini.
3. Mix all the dry ingredients together in a separate bowl.
4. Add in the zucchini wet mixture and mix thoroughly.
5. Grease an 8-inch bundt pan and pour in the bread mix.
6. Pour 1 ½ cups of water into your Instant Pot and lower in the trivet.
7. Place the bundt pan on top of the trivet.
8. Secure the lid.
9. Choose the "Manual" setting and cook for 25 minutes on "high pressure."
10. When done, turn off the cooker and wait 10 minutes.
11. Carefully open the lid and remove the pan.
12. Cool before serving.

Nutritional Info (1 / 24 of recipe):

Total calories - 221
Protein - 4.4
Carbs - 28.1
Fiber - 1.6
Fat - 11

Chocolate-Chip Cheesecake w/ Brownie Crust

Serves: 6
Time: 6 hours, 50 minutes

This cheesecake is decadent without being overwhelming. The brownie crust is rich and delicious, while the filling is light and studded with just enough chocolate chips. Note that this recipe needs to stay in the cooker for 6 hours after it's been cooked; this is the important "water bath" stage that ensures the cheesecake is evenly-cooked and smooth.

Ingredients:

2 eggs
2 cups of water
½ cup butter
½ cup sugar
¾ cup white flour
¼ cup cocoa powder
2 tablespoons honey
¾ teaspoon baking powder
¼ teaspoon salt

24-ounces of softened cream cheese
14-ounces of sweetened condensed milk
3 eggs
½ cup chocolate chips
2 teaspoons vanilla

Directions:

1. Melt the butter and mix in cocoa powder.
2. Cool.
3. Mix the flour, baking powder, sugar, and salt together.
4. Beat the eggs, not too much, and add to the sugar/flour mixture along with the honey and butter/cocoa.
5. Mix everything well.
6. Grease an 8-inch springform pan and pour in the brownie batter.
7. Cover completely with foil.

8. Pour 2 cups of water into the Instant Pot and lower in the trivet.
9. Place the pan on top of the trivet and lock the lid.
10. Cook on "high" for 35 minutes.
11. While this cooks, make your cheesecake filling.
12. Beat the cream cheese until smooth and fluffy.
13. Slowly beat in the sweetened condensed milk until just combined.
14. Add the eggs and vanilla.
15. Mix again until just combined; cheesecake fillings should not be overmixed, or they get holes.
16. Add chocolate chips.
17. Once the brownie crust is done, quick-release the pressure.
18. Remove the pan, unwrap it, and pour the filling on top.
19. Don't wrap the pan again in foil, just lower back into the cooker and secure the lid.
20. Cook for another 15 minutes on "high pressure."
21. When time is up, the Instant Pot should switch to the "keep warm" setting. Check to make sure.
22. Do not touch the Pot for 6 hours.
23. When ready, take out the cheesecake and let it cool.
24. Chill in the fridge before enjoying!

Nutritional Info:

Total calories - 184
Protein - 3.2
Carbs - 18
Fiber - 0
Fat - 11.2

Graham-Cracker Crust Lemon Cheesecake

Serves: 6
Time: 4 hours, 15 minutes

If you love cheesecake, but want a break from chocolate, the beautiful lemon flavors in this recipe are perfect. It has that amazing graham-cracker crust that I love about so many cheesecakes, too.

Ingredients:

½ cup finely-crushed graham cracker crumbs
2 tablespoons sugar
2 tablespoons melted butter

32-ounces of room-temperature cream cheese
3 big eggs
½ cup sugar
1 tablespoon fresh-squeezed lemon juice
2 tablespoons of flour (optional - if you want a denser cake)
1 teaspoon grated lemon zest
½ teaspoon pure vanilla extract
Pinch of salt

Directions:

1. Put the graham cracker crumbs in a bowl and mix in the melted butter and sugar.
2. Take your 7-inch springform pan and coat the sides with the crust mixture on the bottom and a little way up on the side. Press down firmly.
3. To make the filling, begin by mixing the cream cheese (softened at room temperature) and sugar until completely smooth.
4. Add the eggs in one at a time and mix.
5. Mix in the lemon zest, lemon juice, salt, and vanilla until just combined. If you're using flour, add it in now and mix.
6. Pour into the pan over the crust.
7. Pour 2 cups of water into the Instant Pot and lower in the trivet.
8. Place the pan on top of the trivet and secure the lid.
9. Select "Manual," and cook on "high pressure" for 15 minutes.

10. After 15 minutes, turn off the cooker and wait 10 minutes.
11. Carefully remove the pan and let the cheesecake cool.
12. If there's water on top, just blot with a napkin.
13. When no longer hot, cover with plastic wrap and refrigerate for at least 4 hours to chill.

Note

Some people have found that 15 minutes is too short for their cheesecake. If when you remove the pan after letting the pressure come down naturally and it's still liquidy, put back into the Instant Pot for another 5 minutes at a time, before another natural-pressure release. It may take some experimenting to find the perfect time, but then you won't have to experiment next time.

Nutritional Info (⅙ recipe):

Total calories - 719
Protein - 13
Carbs - 34
Fiber - 0
Fat - 60

Greek Yogurt Cheesecake

Serves: 8
Time: 45 minutes (+ 6 hour cooling time)

Cheesecake is a decadent treat, but it's made lower-calorie when you use healthy Greek yogurt in addition to the traditional cream cheese. The result is a simple, vanilla cheesecake with a graham-cracker crust.

Ingredients:

1 ½ cups graham-cracker finely-ground crumbs
1 ½ cups whole-milk Greek yogurt
4-ounces softened, regular cream cheese
4 tablespoons melted butter
2 big eggs
¼ cup sugar
1 teaspoon vanilla

Directions:

1. Mix the cracker crumbs with melted butter.
2. Press down into the bottom of a 7-inch springform pan, so the bottom is covered and the crust is halfway up the pan.
3. Mix the cream cheese, sugar, yogurt, and vanilla until very smooth.
4. Add the eggs one at a time and mix. Be careful not to overmix.
5. Pour into the pan, covering the crust completely up the sides.
6. Lower a trivet into the pressure cooker, along with 1 cup of water.
7. Put the pan on the trivet and lock the lid.
8. Select "Manual," and then 30 minutes on "high pressure."
9. When time is up, hit "Cancel" and wait for the pressure to come down on its own.
10. Carefully open the lid.
11. With a paper towel, blot any excess moisture from the cake.
12. Take out the cake and let it cool on the counter for 1-2 hours.
13. Chill in the fridge for at least 4 hours before serving.

Nutritional Info (⅛ serving):
Total calories - 280   Fiber - 1
Protein - 6   Fat - 9
Carbs - 26

Ricotta + Ginger Cheesecake

Serves: 8
Time: About 45 minutes

Using ricotta gives cheesecake a less cloyingly-sweet taste, as well as a slightly different texture. It's not as silky-smooth, but more cakey. The candied ginger and gingersnap crust also gives the cheesecake a unique, sophisticated flavor, which will surprise and impress any tasters.

Ingredients:

1 ¼ cups gingersnap crumbs
8-ounces softened, regular cream cheese
8-ounces ricotta
5 tablespoons melted and cooled butter
2 big, room-temperature eggs
½ cup packed light brown sugar
¼ cup minced candied ginger
2 tablespoons plain, whole-milk (non-Greek) yogurt
1 tablespoon flour
1 teaspoon vanilla

Directions:

1. Pour 2 cups of water into the Instant Pot and lower in the trivet.
2. Mix butter and gingersnap crumbs.
3. Grease a 7-inch springform pan.
4. Press in the crumb mixture on the bottom and halfway up the pan's sides.
5. In a food processor, mix cream cheese, brown sugar, and ricotta until smooth.
6. As the machine runs, add in eggs one at a time.
7. When it's totally mixed, add in yogurt, and blend again.
8. Using a garlic press, squeeze the candied ginger into the food processor and blend till smooth.
9. Add in flour and vanilla, and mix.
10. Pour into the cheesecake pan.
11. Put the pan on top of the trivet in the Instant Pot.
12. Lock and secure the lid.

13. Press "Manual," and then 25 minutes at "high pressure."
14. When time is up, hit "Cancel" and wait for the pressure to come down naturally.
15. Take out the cheesecake and cool for 1 hour.
16. Remove from the pan and cool in the fridge for at least 6 hours.

Nutritional Info (⅛ serving):

Total calories - 330
Protein - 6
Carbs -17
Fiber - 1
Fat - 27

Sea-Salt Dulce de Leche

Serves: 8
Time: 40 minutes (+ overnight cooling time)

This sweet dessert is created when condensed milk is slowly heated and transformed into a caramel-like sauce. Without a pressure cooker, it can take 2-3 hours. With the Instant Pot, however, it only takes a total of 30 minutes or so, plus an overnight cooling time.

Ingredients:

15-ounce can of sweetened condensed milk
½ teaspoon sea salt
½ teaspoon pure vanilla extract

Directions:

1. Take the label off the milk can, but don't open it.
2. Put the steam rack into your Instant Pot and lower in the milk can so it doesn't touch the sides.
3. Pour enough water into the pot so the can is totally submerged.
4. Close the lid.
5. Press "Manual" and then 20 minutes at "high pressure."
6. When time is up, hit "Cancel" and wait 10 minutes for the pressure to come down.
7. Open the pot lid, but don't touch anything.
8. Let it sit overnight.
9. The next day, open the milk can and pour into a bowl.
10. Whisk in the vanilla and salt.
11. Serve on ice cream, waffles, cake, and so on.

Nutritional Info (¼ cup serving):

Total calories - 171
Protein - 4
Carbs - 29
Fiber - 0
Fat - 3

Orange-Chocolate Bread Pudding

Serves: 4-5
Time: 40 minutes

Orange and chocolate is one of my favorite flavor combinations. It reminds me of Christmas! This rich bread pudding, with the orange zest, dark chocolate, and cream, encompasses all those happy feelings.

Ingredients:

2 cups water
3 ½ cups stale French bread, cut into ¾-inch pieces
3 big eggs
3-ounces chopped dark chocolate
¾ cups heavy cream
½ cup whole milk
⅓ cup sugar + 1 tablespoon
Zest and juice of one orange
1 teaspoon butter
1 teaspoon almond extract
Pinch of salt

Directions:

1. Pour water into the Instant Pot and insert the steamer rack.
2. Grease a 6-7 inch round baking dish.
3. In a bowl, mix the eggs and ⅓ cup of sugar.
4. Pour in the milk, cream, almond extract, orange juice, orange zest, and salt.
5. Mix.
6. Toss the bread pieces in the mixture. Let it soak for 5 minutes.
7. Add the chopped chocolate and stir.
8. Pour in the baking dish and make sure all the bread is submerged.
9. Sprinkle on 1 tablespoon of sugar.
10. Put on the steamer rack (do *not* wrap in foil) and close the lid.
11. Hit "Manual" and cook for 15 minutes on "high pressure."
12. When time is up, hit "Cancel" and wait for the pressure to come down by itself.
13. When depressurized, open the lid and take out the pudding.

14. Serve!

Nutritional Info:

Total calories - 467
Protein - 12
Carbs - 51
Fiber - 1
Fat - 14

Mini Pumpkin Puddings

Serves: 4

Time: 35 minutes (1 ½ hours cooling time)

Love pumpkin pie? These personal-sized pumpkin puddings taste like pie filling, but are much lower in calories and easy to make. Be sure to use real pumpkin puree, not canned pumpkin filling.

Ingredients:

1 cup water
1 cup pumpkin puree
¼ cup sugar
¼ cup half-and-half
1 egg yolk
1 beaten egg
1 tablespoon butter

½ teaspoon ground cinnamon
½ teaspoon pure vanilla extract
¼ teaspoon ground ginger
¼ teaspoon salt
Pinch ground cloves

Directions:

1. Pour the water into the Instant Pot and lower in the steam rack.
2. Grease four heat-safe mugs.
3. In a bowl, whisk the sugar, pumpkin, and spices together.
4. Add the egg, egg yolk, vanilla, and half-and half, and whisk until thoroughly blended.
5. Pour into the containers.
6. Place on the steam rack in the Instant Pot.
7. Lock the lid.
8. Press "Manual," and select 15 minutes on "high pressure."
9. When the timer goes off, hit "Cancel" and wait for the pressure to go down on its own.
10. Open the lid.
11. Wait till the steam dissipates before taking out the puddings.
12. Cool for 1 ½ hours on the counter.

Nutritional Info (¼ serving):

Carbs - 18
Total calories - 174
Protein - 4

Fiber - 1
Fat - 6

Blueberry-Peach Cobbler

Serves: 4-6
Time: 35 minutes

Get ready to make the easiest cobbler of your life. You use frozen peaches and blueberries, so even if they're out of season, you can still get your fruity fix. After making the dough, which doesn't require any kneading, you just plop dumplings of it on top of the thawed fruit and other ingredients, and close up the pressure cooker.

Ingredients:

2 cups peeled, sliced frozen peaches
2 cups frozen blueberries
1 cup flour
⅓ cup buttermilk
⅓ cup sugar + 1 tablespoon
⅓ cup water
2 tablespoons cubed cold butter
1 tablespoon cornstarch
1 ½ teaspoons baking powder
1 teaspoon lime juice
½ teaspoon salt
¼ teaspoon baking soda
Pinch of nutmeg

Directions:

1. In a bowl, mix flour, 1 tablespoon of sugar, baking soda, baking powder, and salt.
2. Add butter and work with your hands to form a cornmeal-like texture.
3. Pour in the buttermilk and mix until just moistened.
4. Form into a dough ball.
5. Hit "sauté" on your Instant Pot and add blueberries, peaches, ⅓ cup sugar, water, lemon juice, cornstarch, and nutmeg.
6. Cook for about 2-3 minutes until the frozen fruit has softened and started to leak juice.
7. Hit "Cancel."

8. Tear 1-inch dough balls out of the big dough ball and put on top of the fruit in the Instant Pot, making about 8 balls in total.
9. Close the lid.
10. Hit "Manual" and select 10 minutes on "high pressure."
11. When time is up, hit "Cancel" and wait for the pressure to decrease naturally.
12. When all the pressure is gone, open the lid and wait a few minutes for the liquid to thicken.
13. Serve!

Nutritional Info:

Total calories - 330
Protein - 5
Carbs - 66
Fiber - 3
Fat - 4

Apple Dumplings

Serves: 6-8
Time: 30 minutes

The fall brings an array of apples and great potential for using your Instant Pot. They say green apples are one of the best kinds for baking, and this recipe proves it. You wrap apple wedges in store-bought crescent roll dough, pop into the cooker with some butter, brown sugar, cider, and autumn spices (nutmeg, cinnamon), and you end up with bite-sized dumplings that everyone will love.

Ingredients:

1 can of crescent rolls
1 big cored, peeled and cut green apple (8 big wedges)
¾ cup apple cider
½ cup brown sugar
4 tablespoons butter
1 teaspoon ground cinnamon
½ teaspoon vanilla extract
Pinch of ground nutmeg

Directions:

1. Hit "Sauté" on your Instant Pot.
2. Prepare the dough by opening the crescent rolls and rolling out flat.
3. Take the apple wedges and wrap each piece in one crescent roll.
4. Put the butter in the pot and hit "Cancel."
5. Throw in the sugar, vanilla, nutmeg, and cinnamon.
6. Stir until everything melts together.
7. Put the dumplings in the pot.
8. Pour the apple cider along the edges of the dumplings.
9. Lock the lid.
10. Press "Manual" and then 10 minutes at "high pressure."
11. When time is done, hit "Cancel" and wait for pressure to come down on its own.
12. Serve dumplings with the cooking liquid spooned on top.

Nutritional Info:

Total calories - 267
Protein - 4
Carbs - 41
Fiber - 2
Fat - 5

Creamy Rice Pudding w/ Golden Raisins

Serves: 6
Time: 15-20 minutes

Rice pudding can be served hot *or* cold, and even eaten for breakfast if you like! When I think about rice pudding, I think about standing over a stovetop for forever, but that's not the case at all with the Instant Pot. This recipe uses golden raisins, which add a lovely sweetness to the pudding.

Ingredients:

5 cups milk
2 eggs
1 ½ cups Arborio rice
1 cup half and half
1 cup golden raisins

¾ cup sugar
1 ½ teaspoons pure vanilla extract
½ teaspoon salt
Cinnamon as desired

Directions:

1. In your Instant Pot, mix rice, salt, sugar, and milk.
2. Select the "sauté" button and bring to a boil while stirring constantly.
3. Once boiling, secure the lid and seal the steam release valve.
4. Press "Rice."
5. Meanwhile, mix eggs, vanilla, and half and half together in a bowl.
6. When the Instant Pot is ready, push "Cancel" and wait 15 minutes.
7. Quick-release any remaining pressure and take off the lid.
8. Pour in the egg mixture and raisins.
9. Push "sauté" again and let the pudding come to a boil, without putting on the lid.
10. Push "Cancel."
11. Serve hot or put in the fridge to chill.
12. Sprinkle on cinnamon.

Nutritional Info (⅙ recipe):
Total calories - 518
Protein - 14
Carbs - 94

Fiber - 0
Fat - 11

Red-Wine Baked Apples

Serves: 6
Time: 30-4o minutes

These grown-up "baked" apples are a perfect way to use up fresh apples during the fall and enhance their natural flavors, whatever variety you're using. The cooking liquid, which you spoon over the baked fruit, is made from red wine and sweetened with sugar and raisins. Don't forget the cinnamon!

Ingredients:

6 cored apples
1 cup red wine
½ cup sugar
¼ cup raisins
1 teaspoon cinnamon

Directions:

1. Set the apples inside the Instant Pot.
2. Pour in wine and add the sugar, cinnamon, and raisins.
3. Secure the lid.
4. Select "Manual" and cook for 10 minutes on "high pressure."
5. When the timer beeps, hit "cancel" and wait 20-30 minutes for the pressure to come down.
6. Serve the apples in a bowl with the cooking liquid spooned over.

Nutritional Info:

Total calories - 188.7
Protein - 0
Carbs - 41.9
Fiber - 3.8
Fat - 0

Cinnamon-Crumble Stuffed Peaches

Serves: 5
Time: About 15 minutes

There's nothing I love more about summer than peaches, so I eat them any way I can, especially dessert! Fresh peaches are steamed in the pressure cooker, and stuffed with an addicting, buttery, cinnamon crumble. You can serve it with a good vanilla ice cream for a frosty contrast, or just eat the peaches as is.

Ingredients:

5 medium-sized peaches
¼ cup brown sugar
¼ cup flour
2 tablespoons butter
½ teaspoon ground cinnamon
1/2 teaspoon pure almond extract + ¼ teaspoon almond extract
Pinch of sea salt

Directions:

1. Carefully slice about ¼ inch off the top of your peaches.
2. With a sharp knife, cut into the top and take out the pits, so the peaches have a little hollow.
3. In a bowl, mix the flour, sugar, cinnamon, and salt.
4. Melt the butter and add, along with the ½ teaspoon of almond extract.
5. Mix until crumbly.
6. Fill peaches.
7. Pour 1 cup of water into the Instant Pot and add ¼ teaspoon of almond extract right into the water.
8. Lower in the steamer basket and arrange the peaches inside.
9. Secure the lid.
10. Press "Manual" and decrease the time to 3 minutes.
11. When the timer sounds, press "Cancel" and unplug.
12. Quick-release the pressure.
13. Remove the peaches with tongs and cool for 10 minutes.
14. Serve with vanilla ice cream or devour as is!

Nutritional Info (1 peach w/ crumble):

Total calories - 162
Protein - 2
Carbs - 30
Fiber - 2.3
Fat - 5

Individual Brownie Cakes

Serves: 4
Time: 28 minutes

Served in ramekins, these little brownie cakes are the perfect amount of chocolatey goodness. With less than 10 ingredients, they're also super easy to put together, and thanks to the Instant Pot, effortlessly moist.

Ingredients:

2 eggs
⅔ cup sugar
½ cup flour
4 tablespoons cocoa powder
4 tablespoons unsalted butter
2 tablespoons chocolate chips
2 tablespoons powdered sugar
¼ teaspoon vanilla extract

Directions:

1. Melt the butter and chocolate chips together in a heatproof bowl.
2. Add the sugar and beat until mixed.
3. Add in the eggs and vanilla and beat again.
4. Sift in the flour and cocoa into the wet ingredients and blend.
5. Pour 1 cup of water into the Instant Pot and insert the steamer rack.
6. Pour the brownie batter into 4 ramekins and cover the top with foil.
7. Lower into the Instant Pot on top of the rack.
8. Select "Manual" and choose "high pressure" for 18 minutes.
9. When time is up, quick-release the pressure.
10. Remove the ramekins and cool for a few minutes.
11. Dust on some powdered sugar and serve!

Nutritional Info (1 cake):

Total calories - 377
Protein - 6
Carbs - 56

Fiber - 0
Fat - 17

Conclusion

The Instant Pot represents what is best about pressure cookers - speed, convenience, and delicious food. It's been a long time since pressure cookers were too expensive or too dangerous, and now with a cooker like the Instant Pot, you can cook just about anything without having to worry about explosions or leaking. Safety features like the locking lid and exhaust valve ensure the cooker won't get started unless it's secure, and it won't become over-pressurized. With a stovetop cooker, you would be responsible for monitoring all that, but with the Instant Pot, it's all automatic.

Hopefully you have a clear idea of how the Instant Pot works and what all those buttons mean. It really isn't too hard once you get started. The recipes all told you what to press and when, so if you follow the instructions, you'll get great results. Just remember to keep your cooker clean, and it will serve you well for years to come.

This book gave you 110 recipes to try out in your Instant Pot, so if you haven't started yet, get cooking! You'll wonder why you didn't start pressure-cooking sooner, and you won't need to buy another rice cooker, slow cooker, or expensive yogurt maker ever again.

VANESSA OLSEN

Index 1 - Converting Slow-Cooker Recipes to Pressure Cookers

There's a lot of demand for converting slow cooker recipes to pressure cookers. A meal that normally takes hours will cook much faster, so it's understandable why people want to adapt their recipes.

The first step is to look at the ingredient list of the slow cooker recipe and cook any aromatics first. Aromatics include any herbs, celery, garlic, carrots, onion, and whole spices like ginger.

The next thing to figure out is how much liquid the slow cooker recipe requires. You'll want to see how much liquid the recipe *ends* with, because pressure cookers don't lose much liquid from beginning to end. Add about ½ cup for your pressure cooker recipe.

Cooking time will be very different. See how long the meal is actually cooking in the slow cooker and reduce it by ⅔. That's the time you'll set for the pressure cooker. The only other thing to be aware of is that slow cookers are often larger than pressure cookers, so be careful not to overfill the Instant Pot. You might need to cut the recipe in half, or cook in two batches.

The other way to find a pressure-cooker version of a favorite slow-cooker recipe is to just google it. Odds are someone has already converted it, and you just have to follow it.

Index 2- Time Charts For Electric Pressure/Stove Top Cookers

The Instant Pot only gets to about 11 PSI, compared to stovetop cookers, which reach 15 PSI. You don't have to do anything different in terms of ingredients or preparation, but the cooking time will be different. Usually adding just a few minutes is enough, though for longer-cooking dishes, you'll add as much as 20 minutes. Here's a handy chart for common pressure-cooker foods:

Food	Electric Pressure Cooker (10-12 psi) Time	Stove top Pressure Cooker (13-15 psi) Time	Pressure Selection
Beef (brisket)	70	50	High
Beef (ground)	6	6	High
Beef (ribs)	60	45	High
Chicken breast (boneless)	1	1	High
Chicken (ground)	5	4	High
Chicken (whole)	20	15	High
Eggs (poached)	2	2	Low

Lamb chops	7	3	High
Pork chops	8	6	High
Pork ribs	20	15	High
Pork sausage	10	8	High
Roast beef (medium)	8 to 10	8	High
Turkey breast (sliced)	7 to 9	7	High
Turkey leg	35	30	High
Fish fillet	3	2	Low
Salmon	6	5	Low
Shrimp	2	1	Low
Trout	12	8	Low
Oats (steel-cut)	3	3	High
Oats (rolled)	10	10	High
Brown rice	20	18	High
Jasmine rice (rinsed)	1	1	Low or high
White (long-grain) rice	3	3	Low or high

Amaranth	8	8	High
Barley flakes	20	18	High
Pearl barley	20	18	High
Buckwheat	2	2	High
Millet	1	1	High
Quinoa	1	1	High
Cabbage	3	3	Low/High
Collards	1	1	Low/High
Eggplant	2-3	2-3	Low/High
Green beans (fresh/frozen)	2-3	2-3	Low/High
Kale	1	1	Low/High
Mushrooms (dry)	10	8	Low/High
Mushrooms (fresh)	5	5	Low/High
Artichoke hearts	3	3	Low or high

Broccoli	3 to 5	3 to 5	Low or high
Carrots (sliced)	1 to 2	1 to 2	Low or high
Cauliflower (florets)	2 to 3	2 to 3	Low or high
Corn on the cob	5	5	Low or high
Onions	3	3	Low or high
Peas (fresh or frozen)	2 to 3	2 to 3	Low or high
Bell peppers	3 to 4	3 to 4	Low or high
Whole sweet potatoes	15	10	High
Butternut squash (halves)	6	6	Low or high
Apples	3	2	High
Blackberries	6	6	High
Cherries	2	2	High
Chestnuts (fresh)	8	5	High

Figs (fresh)	3	3	Low/High

Figs (dried)	8	6	Low/High
Peaches (whole/fresh)	4	2	High
Black beans (soaked)	6	4	High
White beans (soaked)	8	6	High
Lentils (dry/regular)	12	10	High
Peas (dry/whole /green)	18	16	High

Thank you so much for reading this book!

I hope the book was able to teach you how pressure cooking can simplify your everyday life.

Finally, if you enjoyed this book, then I'd like to ask you for a favor, would you be kind enough to leave a review for this book on Amazon? It'd be greatly appreciated!

Preview of Mediterranean Diet Cookbook: 105 Easy, Irresistible, and Healthy Recipes for Weight Loss and Improved Quality of Life While Minimizing the Risk of Disease

In today's day and age, there is a lengthy list of diets which people can't adhere to for one main reason: it's just a diet! People will begin a diet with high hopes of improved health and better quality of life only to lose their way in a confusing set of guidelines and numbers. Sound familiar?

If it does, I'm *glad* a diet has failed you before. It only means you'll see the true worth of the Mediterranean diet – a diet which has little to do with number crunching and non-human eating strategies, but instead revolves around creating a life full of good food, healthy relationships, happiness, and longevity.

Indeed, the Mediterranean diet is about so much more than the kinds of foods you're eating. It comes as no surprise though, when we think about the lively, vibrant people who inhabit the Mediterranean region. Not only are their lives full, but they're healthy, too. And good health is one of the greatest blessings known to mankind.

And these people aren't healthy because they eat bird food day in and day out. These people are healthy because they've mastered the art of moderation. A little bit of this, a little bit of that, a little bit of love, and a little bit of fat. They create colorful, nutritious, and well balanced meals which contribute to their lives of ease and simplicity. It's all about focusing on getting the good stuff in us, and mixing it with little bits of indulgence. And that's exactly what this cookbook is about, too.

Upon flipping through the pages of this book you will encounter recipes of all types – some savory, some nutritious, yet all of them delicious. This cookbook focuses on creating a healthy lifestyle focused on spending time with loved ones and living every day to the fullest, just as the people of the Mediterranean region do best.

Not only are the recipes in this book absolutely delicious, but as the title reads, they will also result in some pretty amazing health benefits. I touch on those within the next couple of chapters, and if you can start to embrace the Mediterranean way of life, you can expect to reap those same benefits!

Welcome to the wonderful world of olive oil, feta cheese, seafood, and of course, wining and dining!

MY OTHER BOOKS

Ketogenic Diet - Achieve Rapid Weight Loss while Gaining Incredible Health and Energy

Ketogenic Diet Cookbook: 80 Easy, Delicious, and Healthy Recipes to Help You Lose Weight, Boost Your Energy, and Prevent Cancer, Stroke and Alzheimer`s

Ketogenic Diet-2 in 1 Box Set-A Complete Guide to the Ketogenic Diet-115 Amazing Recipes for Weight Loss and Improved Health

Mediterranean Diet for Beginners-50 Amazing Recipes for Weight Loss and Improved Health

Mediterranean Diet-2 in 1 Box Set: A Comprehensive Guide to the Mediterranean Diet-155 Mouth-Watering and Healthy Recipes to Help You Lose Weight, Increase Your Energy Level and Prevent Disease

30 Days of Whole Food: 120 Irresistible and Healthy Recipes-A 30 Day Whole Food Challenge That Will Help You Lose Weight, Boost Your Metabolism, and Prevent Disease

Pressure Cooker Cookbook: 100 Quick, Easy, and Healthy Pressure Cooker Recipes for Nourishing and Delicious Meals

Pressure Cooker Cookbook: 110 Quick, Easy, and Delicious Pressure Cooker Recipes for Electric and Stove Top Pressure

Cookers

Electric Pressure Cooker Cookbook: 60 Quick, Easy, and Healthy Pressure Cooker Recipes for Electric Pressure Cookers

Electric Pressure Cooker Cookbook: 100 Quick, Easy, and Healthy Pressure Cooker Recipes for Electric Pressure Cookers

Pressure Cooker Cookbook: 2 in 1 Box Set-200 Mouth-Watering and Healthy Pressure Cooker Recipes for Stove Top and Electric Pressure Cookers

Pressure Cooker Cookbook: 3 in 1 Box Set-310 Mouth-Watering and Healthy Pressure Cooker Recipes for Stove Top and Electric Pressure Cookers

Pressure Cooker Cookbook: 370 Quick, Easy, and Healthy Pressure Cooker Recipes for Amazingly Tasty and Nourishing Meals

I would love to give you a gift. Please visit happyhealthycookingonline.com to get these 4 amazing eBooks for free!

Please visit my blog happyhealthycookingonline.com for more awesome recipes and helpful content.

Thank you and good luck!

19478060R00119

Printed in Great Britain
by Amazon